a cra
occupation

For my family

a crazy
occupation

Eyewitness to the intifada

Jamie Tarabay

ALLEN&UNWIN

First published in 2005

Allen & Unwin
83 Alexander Street
Crows Nest NSW 2065
Australia
Phone: (61 2) 8425 0100
Fax: (61 2) 9906 2218
Email: info@allenandunwin.com
Web: www.allenandunwin.com

National Library of Australia
Cataloguing-in-Publication entry:

Tarabay, Jamie.
   A crazy occupation: eyewitness to the intifada.

   Includes index.
   ISBN 1 74114 650 X.

   1. Tarabay, Jamie. 2. Journalists – Australia – Biography.
   3. Arab-Israeli conflict. 4. Israel – Description and
   travel. 5. Israel – Politics and government – 1993– . I.
   Title

070.92

Set in 12/14.5 Cochin by Midland Typesetters
Printed by McPherson's Printing Group, Maryborough, Victoria

10 9 8 7 6 5 4 3 2 1

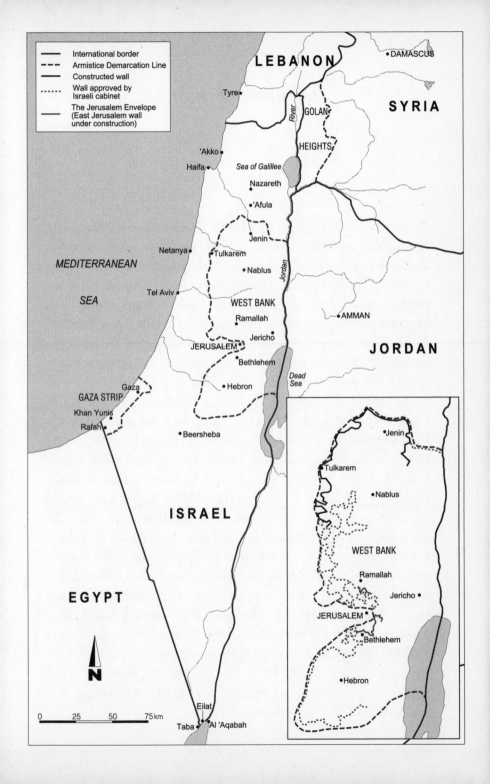

Acknowledgments

I am above all grateful to Morag Ramsay, my frighteningly efficient and dear friend, who got this whole process started. I am indebted to the indefatigable and indulgent Richard Walsh. I thank Ted Anthony for giving me his time, support and constant inspiration, and I thank John Van Tiggelen for his enchanted perspective. I thank Anna Sathiah, Mark Dapin and Will Swanton, who I struggled to share the first few pages with and who all immediately urged me to carry on. Thank you to the editors at The Associated Press who helped make this happen, including Deborah Seward, Karin Laub, Dan Perry and Jocelyn Noveck. I am grateful to Jo Paul and everyone at Allen & Unwin for their guidance, happy energy and endless patience. To my Jerusalem friends: Lizzie Dalziel, Jason Keyser, Chloe Edwards, Lulu Navarro, James Hider, Kylie Morris, Enric Marti and Yoav Appel, I am proud to have worked, lived, cried and laughed with you. To everyone in the Jerusalem bureau, especially Haitham Hamad, Ibrahim H and Ibrahim B and Mohammed Daragh-meh, I will always be grateful. To the many other talented and incredible people I have been privileged to know who helped shape this narrative over the past five years, I thank you. Thank you to my friends, especially Penny Spink and Emma Tinkler, for being unstinting in their encouragement and love. My parents George and Leila, and my sisters Christine, Maria and Stefanie, have never stopped loving and supporting me, and to them I owe my greatest thanks.

Contents

Atchany, Lebanon
October 1989–July 1990

i'd be fast asleep most times. On other nights I could just make it out, the faint boom, then another, then another, growing louder and louder. I'd shove the pillow over my head and shut my eyes tight, thinking, *If I ignore the sound it will go away.* But the booms just got louder. Sons of bitches.

'Come on, Maria, Jamie, Christine. Come on, we're going downstairs,' my mother would call as she poked her head into the room. It usually happened at three in the morning. Maria would be the first to get up. Christine was always the last. Unlike me, she never needed to pretend to be asleep. Her slumber was always deep and untroubled. She could grind her teeth in her sleep and wake up everyone else, yet sleep on oblivious.

'Get up,' I'd say, kicking the foot of her mattress, resenting every last moment she lay there with her eyes shut.

Changing into track pants, we'd gather pillows, blankets, a deck of cards and head down to the bomb shelter in our building. Every family had its own area staked out with their mattresses on fold-out beds, pillows, cushions and other bedding to keep out the cold. Most of the people lived in the buildings across the street so they spent the entire night in the shelter, unlike our family; we went down there only when we could hear the explosions. I'd smother the urge to throw up as I inhaled the familiar fetid smell of sleep exhaled by dozens of old men and babies as they slumbered.

The space in the shelter was big enough for two three-bedroom apartments and a dusty corridor linked it to the building next door. This meant the residents of that building could wander into our shelter and vice versa, so the adults could socialise during the night. There were about ten families in the shelter, most with young children. There was a ping-pong table in one corner and a television set, where people would watch an Egyptian soap opera if the reception wasn't too scratchy. Sometimes we'd play cards with some of the other kids in the building but Mum and Dad never let us play if there were too many guys at the table. The constant cigarette smoke used to make Christine's asthma worse. She was always coughing. I don't know where people went to the toilet; it wasn't something I wanted to think about. I didn't need to, since we could go upstairs to our apartment, no matter how severe the bombing.

One of the families had put up cardboard barriers between them and the rest of the shelter because they thought they were better than everyone else. The daughter of that family had a new car and new clothes and flashy jewellery; she called herself Coco. She always wore make-up and kept her hair styled, as though she were about to head out for a night on the town, and she never appeared in her pyjamas. Her younger brother also had some ridiculous nickname. It was a very snobbish Lebanese thing to do, give yourself a French nickname to justify your pretentious credentials. A Roula would be called Roro, Josephine would be JouJou, Francois would be FouFou. It was too French, too froufrou, too fraudulent. What was wrong with your real name?

We used to sit in our corner sniggering at one man who snored so loudly that he'd keep everyone else awake. We'd entertain ourselves by doing little riffs in between the snores, like music. We called him 'Fanore', joining his first name to 'snore'. We got into trouble once for making too much noise — some of the other kids were giggling with us and my father overheard. He shushed us in case Fanore woke up and clued onto the fun we were making out of his rhythmic wheezing. Sometimes it was the only entertainment we had. Couldn't sleep now.

I'd go nuts from boredom. Electricity was minimal so the lighting was weak and I couldn't read, especially if everyone else was trying to sleep. I'd try not to laugh out loud nervously whenever some of the bombs sounded like they had landed close by. Once Coco had a panic attack and started screaming and crying, afraid we were going to be hit.

'We're all going to die!' she screeched. *Wrong*, I thought. *You're going to die, not me. This is your country, you belong here, I don't. It's not my time to die.* I never felt like I was ever in any real danger, even though houses nearby were hit. I just didn't believe that we were going to die here, in Lebanon. I was defiant.

We lived like this, on and off, for ten months. No school. No travelling. Nothing. During daytime walks around the village, people would look at us, point and say, 'Those are the Australian girls,' then stare at us as we, pretending not to care or notice, continued on. *You laugh at the way we speak Arabic. You think the way we speak to each other is funny, even though you can't understand. We could be talking about you and your funny haircut and you would never know.* We weren't snobs. We just didn't belong.

The guys in the village would attempt to talk to us, trying not to be deterred by our domineering father even though we ourselves were afraid of his disapproval. If they saw us walking in the street they would offer us flowers or try to start conversations. Once I was at the local pizzeria waiting for my order when a group of guys came in and sat at a table. I was talking to Rita, who was working behind the counter that day, when someone thrust a white gardenia in my face.

'Would you accept this flower from me?' a guy asked in English. I couldn't even turn around to look at him I was so embarrassed. I knew everyone was watching. I shook my head and said no.

'Why not?' he asked. I just shook my head again and looked at Rita, who was laughing now. The guy gave up and turned away, but when he saw my father later that day he told him he'd tried to give me a flower.

'What did she do?' my father asked the boy.

'She refused to take it,' he said.

'Good,' my father replied, nodding approvingly.

Each day was the same: stay at home; watch one of the 20 Kung Fu movies we'd hired and already seen a thousand times before; write stories; listen to Kylie Minogue because she was Australian and so were we; sleep. Then wake up in the middle of the night to go downstairs again. Sometimes, standing out on the balcony of our apartment, I'd look across and see Um Assad, our neighbour, lighting candles and placing them on the rail.

'This one's so Hafez al-Assad will get cancer,' she'd yell, venting her anger at Syria's president for his relentless bombing campaign.

The radios were switched onto Liban Tel, a local station

that played rousing songs about Beirut, Lebanon or the Lebanese army non-stop. Tens of thousands of people had set up camp outside Baabda, the presidential palace in Beirut where General Michel Aoun, the Maronite leader, was holed up, when reports that the Syrians might bomb him started. We watched the demonstrations on television. People would shout, 'With our souls and our blood, we'll redeem you, General,' waiting for him to come out onto the balcony to wave at them and make a speech.

When school started again, albeit briefly, the teachers organised a day trip to the palace as a school excursion. The only other excursion we had was when we went to the snow. In the whole three years we were there we only went on these two school field trips.

How did we get here? My father, with his love–hate relationship with his father, took us from Australia to Lebanon, then back to Australia. Then to Germany, where five of our uncles lived, and to Australia. Then to Lebanon again. And again. It was his desperate urge for a nod of approval from a man who never gave it, coupled with a ferocious loyalty to his long-suffering mother—our grandmother—that made my father the lost and forever prodigal son, and us the cargo that was shipped back and forth between ports.

Like his brothers, my father left Lebanon to try and make a living in a country with greater economic opportunities. Some of them travelled to Sweden, Germany, Switzerland and the United States. They always returned to give the rest of the family, struggling on little money, part of their earnings. But none felt the pull of home stronger than my father, who initially had worked all over the Middle East as a car mechanic. He chose to migrate to Australia, the furthest place from Lebanon, because of his desire to get away from his father. Yet he always returned, seeking approval, and always left because he never got it.

I vaguely remember my mother telling us about our 1978 trip to Lebanon, which ended after war broke out again. At the time, my parents had bought an apartment, furnished it, and prepared to live in Lebanon permanently. Christine was only weeks old; I was three. Maria, who was four, set fire to my grandparents' living room and ran out, leaving me to take the blame. I was my grandfather's favourite, so I didn't get yelled at. To this day everyone believes I was the one who held the candle to the curtain and then just stood there and watched as the flames licked the walls. Another snapshot image in my mind from that time is of a tank going by in my grandparents' street. My mother said we left Lebanon then with only the clothes on our backs, leaving the apartment, the furniture, everything, to return to Australia.

In July 1987, we arrived back in Beirut on a stinking hot day, still clad in the jeans and stifling sweaters we'd worn on the flight from Australia, where it was winter. We were here to stay, Dad had told us. This time, it was for good. We would live here, go to school—Australia wasn't home any more. This would be home from now on. I was twelve and all four of us girls were still young enough to be able to adapt and learn. But it was hard. We had so many relatives—my father was one of thirteen children—and we struggled to keep track of them.

It was hardly our only struggle though. We struggled to understand the culture. Struggled to know what it meant to be a Christian in a Lebanon that was being overtaken by political forces I didn't understand. What twelve-year-old does? Who were the Phalange? Who were the Gemayels? The Shamouns? The Franjiyahs? We couldn't go north because the Syrians were there, we were told. The Israelis were in the south. The Muslims were in the west of Beirut and the Christians in the east.

My father hated that we went to school with boys. We had gone to an all-girls Catholic school back in Sydney and that had been just fine for my strict, overprotective practising Catholic father. He didn't want us to be in a situation he couldn't control. Or maybe he just knew what boys were like—after all, he was one once. He had searched in vain every school in east Beirut, from the mountains to the seaside towns, to find one that taught only girls—we eventually went to a Seventh Day Adventist School as it was the only one that taught maths and science in English; the Catholic schools taught them in French. He couldn't bear the thought that we would have to sit in class all day with boys he didn't know. He would drop us off and pick us up promptly every day. As he collected us one afternoon, he saw a boy I liked watching me as I got into the car. I shrank down in my seat as he called the boy over, embarrassment crawling across my twelve-year-old face like a red rash. He asked: 'Is there anything you want to say to my daughter?'

'No,' answered the terrified boy, shaking his head as he stepped away from the car. The boy never spoke to me again after that day. I was shattered.

On 14 March 1989, Christine's birthday, Dad was taking us to school and as usual we stopped on our way to get mana'eesh, the thin pizza-like dough topped with zaatar (a mix of sesame, oregano and other herbs) or cheese. When we turned into our school's street Maria spotted a boy from her class coming towards us on his Vespa. We slowed down and he leaned into our car, his bike swaying beneath him, and yelled excitedly, 'There's no school today. The Syrians are bombing!'

We all froze. *Really? Bombing? Here? Now?* We hadn't heard anything. We'd never had the full-on experience of war before. My father drove on undaunted, swinging into the school's car park. Teachers were waving madly, telling the swarming students and cars to go back. My father quickly turned the car around and sped all the way home to our little village. We spent the next ten months descending most nights to the bomb shelter and returning to our home in the morning.

In the middle of the new hostilities my father managed to secure our exit, risking a trip to Beirut to organise the plane tickets. During one short lull on a stinking hot day in July 1990, we sped to the airport, leaving Lebanon and returning to Sydney. I couldn't get out of there fast enough. For me, the Middle East was over. Its violence, its convoluted geography and its deadly passions were more than I could bear. I never thought I would willingly go back again and live there and, more than that, actually care about the people and their destiny.

Then I regained my senses again
And looked into my heart to find/

That I believe that one fine day all the children of Abraham
Will lay down their swords forever in Jerusalem.

'Jerusalem', Steve Earle

PART ONE

hitting the
pause button

CHAPTER ONE

September 2000

there was a wail at the other end of the line. I closed my eyes and gripped the phone tighter.

'Well, your mother's fainted,' my father said. 'Do you really have to go? Don't you understand? We'll never be able to go to Lebanon again. Please don't go, please Jamie, please.'

It was not a good start. I was only tentatively suggesting to my parents that The Associated Press (AP) had offered me a job in the Middle East, namely in Jerusalem. I wanted to gauge their reaction. What I hadn't told them was that I'd virtually accepted the position of an Arabic-speaking reporter, covering the Palestinian territories.

I was already agonising over the decision. I'd never been there before and had no idea what to expect. The Israeli–Palestinian conflict was never something that particularly interested me. When the option came in high school to study it, we all chose the Russian revolution instead. It just appeared tidier; a revolution that had a natural conclusion that we could study in its full and complete context.

The Arab–Israeli conflict seemed like one big headache and far too complicated for our high school minds. We didn't want to solve the world's problems, we just wanted to study a gripping time in history and do well enough to get into university. I didn't even know what the West Bank was, let alone where it was. Camp David, Oslo, the Palestinian Authority, Areas A, B and C—they may as well have been elements in a science experiment. They would have made as much sense to me.

I could understand my parents' anxiety. They originally left Lebanon before war broke out in 1975. From afar they had watched as their beloved Beirut was violated by warring militias and rampaging soldiers from different invading countries and domestic factions. It still breaks my father's heart that we will never know the Beirut they knew, the one they called the Paris of the Middle East, where my mother as a teenager used to hitch rides with her friends to buy their bell-bottomed jeans at men's stores and stop traffic in their micro mini skirts.

We'd gone back several times when my sisters and I were younger—we lived in a village 40 minutes out of Beirut for three years from 1987 to 1990. During those ten months of which we spent most nights in a bomb shelter, our understanding was that the Syrians were bombing everything. But like most childhood memories, things were not as they seemed.

The conflict that erupted in 1989 began with the Syrians bombing the Lebanese, but soon after domestic rivalries led to the Lebanese army, headed by General Michel Aoun, fighting Samir Geagea and the Lebanese Forces. Declared truces were never honoured and ceasefires held for only hours at a time. It soon turned into a war between Geagea's Forces and the army led by Aoun.

Locked away in our tiny village sandwiched between Bikfaya and Beirut, we had not been as exposed to the killings as others. An army base in the valley below us did make our little village a target for rockets, but we would just stop in our tracks if we were hiking in the hills whenever we heard a missile scream overhead. We never thought to take cover; we just waited to see where it would land.

When we returned to Sydney in July 1990, my three sisters and I focused on finishing school and we put our time in Lebanon behind us. We had always felt like foreigners in a strange land, where our attempts to speak the language with our heavy Australian accents were met with amusement. My elder sister was so upset by the teasing in Lebanon that she stopped speaking Arabic unless absolutely necessary.

I really shouldn't have expected any lesser reaction from my parents to my news now. Unlike many of their friends, they weren't your average, overly hysterical and prone-to-drama Lebanese people. They'd done enough and seen enough during their lifetime to harden themselves against bad news. They knew enough for me to know they weren't being ridiculous for the sake of it. Still, they weren't helping. When they asked me why I wanted to go to Israel, I didn't know where to start.

I knew I desperately wanted out of Singapore, where I was phoning them from. My relationship with my boyfriend—the reason why I had come to Singapore in the first place—had crumbled. We weren't even talking to each other any more. The end of our time together had felt like a divorce to me. After going out for a couple of years, we'd moved to Singapore together, bought furniture and planned to marry. It had taken ages for my parents to agree to my going. When everything collapsed, I was completely unprepared for the emotional turmoil that overtook me.

I wasn't happy in my job. I'd already applied for positions in Cairo and Sydney before I was approached with this offer. I didn't know anything about Israel but I thought it would be a good kick-start to my career as a foreign correspondent. The situation seemed stable enough. I had a romantic notion of wandering up and down the narrow alleyways of the Old City, writing features on the peace process and how everyone was getting along.

My parents, on the other hand, thought my going to Israel was complete madness, even though there was nothing to suggest it was dangerous. Indeed, when I interviewed for the position, the political leaders involved had just concluded a summit at Camp David on a seemingly positive note. By all accounts the Palestinians were still expected to declare statehood on 13 September 2000. But, to alleviate my parents' anxiety, I made some inquiries.

I contacted several people who'd worked in Jerusalem and whose backgrounds were similar to mine, to seek their opinions and hear about their experiences. I spoke to one AP reporter who was from Lebanon and had worked mainly in Gaza during her tenure in Israel. She said it had gone well for her and that being an Australian, I shouldn't have a problem. Confident I was making the right decision, I flew home to Sydney for a week of major public relations with my family, to try to convince *them* that everything would be fine.

I sat with my father in the backyard and went over my reasons with him for doing this: something new, something different, a good opportunity for my career. He reluctantly accepted my going but he didn't want any of their Lebanese friends to know about it. For some Lebanese people 'Israel' was a dirty word. People never talked about the place. They were afraid Syrian intelligence would turn their whisper into an accusation of an Israeli connection, which might herald charges of espionage and generally make life unpleasant for them and their friends and relatives. It was only when my Uncle Chris rang from Germany, heard the news and got totally excited about it that my father began to view things differently.

'I've always wanted to go scuba diving in the Red Sea,' my uncle told me over the phone. 'Now I have the perfect reason to go.' When he spoke to my father, Uncle Chris said he wasn't at all surprised by my resolve.

'Yes, she's an adventurer, she's a Tarabay, you're right,' my father agreed with him, responding to this theme. Now that my Uncle Chris had put a positive spin on things, my father was more willing to not only accept the idea but to urge my mother to view it in a more encouraging way. They got excited about the fact that I would soon be seeing the Old City.

'It's every Christian's wish to go to Jerusalem,' Dad said to me, and here I was with the chance to live and work there. I was so relieved. I could go now without having to worry about my family. But that didn't make it easier to leave.

I was still getting used to being on my own. I couldn't stop crying when I said goodbye to my parents and my sisters at Sydney Airport. I clung tightly to my mother as we both cried. I didn't want to let her go. In the end I turned away and kept walking towards the immigration counter, with my father following me as far as he was allowed to go. Once I passed through I ran to the toilets and locked myself in a stall, trying to control my tears.

I returned to Singapore to finish packing and to make my final preparations to leave the tiny island where I'd lived and worked for fifteen months. I was more than ready to leave; I'd made some good friends and it was here that I first joined the AP, but it wouldn't be easy for me to live here now without thinking of my doomed relationship, and that only depressed me.

As I left the Royal Thai Airways flight at Bangkok and went to catch my connecting El Al flight to Tel Aviv on 18 September 2000, I followed the signs to my gate and ran smack into a long line of passengers as weary as I was. There were two signs and two queues—one for foreigners and one for Israelis. The Israeli passengers, brandishing blue passports, swept through security after answering the Israeli security people's questions. Everyone in my queue was held up for at least half an hour.

'What are you doing in Israel?'

'Where will you be staying?'

'With whom will you be staying?'

'Do you have any relatives in Israel?'

'Where will you be working?'

'Do you have any kind of documentation to show that they're expecting you?'

'Do you have a contact number?'

I did. And the security officer called the AP office in Jerusalem, where it was 9 p.m.—it was past 1 a.m. in Bangkok and I'd been on the go since the previous morning. Since I also have the misfortune of not being able to sleep on planes I was in exceedingly rough shape by then but I managed to remain patient. More than anything else I was curious at all the questions.

After a fifteen-hour flight that could have been halved had El Al, the Israeli airline, not had a policy of avoiding the air space of countries it considered hostile to Israel, I arrived in Tel Aviv. There were more questions at the airport but by this stage (after still having had no sleep) I was beyond curious, beyond bored. I was exasperated. I remember standing at the baggage carousel watching the Israeli passengers crowd the conveyor belt, all wanting to get their luggage first. I stood there slightly bemused but intimidated. The Israelis seemed to me to be even pushier than the Singaporeans. I'd been warned about Israeli manners, or lack of them, before I left. But I didn't really know what to expect. What surprised me after I arrived there and settled in was how many Israelis themselves conceded that yes, theirs was a rude-ish culture, for so many reasons, nervous anxiety, stress, existentialism — all things that I would soon confront myself.

I barely glimpsed Tel Aviv as my taxi sped away from the airport on a highway that passed an industrial site and stretched towards green hills in the distance. I stared out the window as the scenery and the atmosphere changed. We were climbing now, the taxi curving along the road as it hugged a hill, driving round and round. I sat up, sensing we were closer and then, on the next curve, it came into view.

'Jerusalem?' I pointed, asking the driver.

'*Ken*,' he said, which meant 'yes'. Then he used the Hebrew word for Jerusalem, '*Yerushalim.*'

I could see only the rooftops of white buildings and a cemetery on the right that seemed to cover the entire hillside. *I'm here*, I thought, as we drew nearer and nearer. *This is history in front of me.*

It was hot, even on this September day. My driver had to ring Tzipi Alpert, the woman who owned the studio apartment the AP had rented for me until I found my own, because he couldn't find the place. When we pulled up she and her husband were standing outside the building, smiling in the bright sunlight. I dumped my suitcases in the tiny studio and quickly showered before heading to the AP office.

I was haggard from jetlag when I first walked into the AP newsroom. The dizzying movements of the people there overwhelmed me. I met my news editor, Karin Laub, who then introduced me to my fellow Arabic desk reporter, Ibrahim Hazboun, and to Haitham Hamad, a senior producer for Associated Press Television News. Haitham took me out for a coffee at the café next door, The Milky Way. I soon discovered that many restaurants and eateries in Jerusalem were dairy and kosher so all thoughts I may have had of pork and seafood had to be relegated to distant memories of Sunday brunches with hung-over friends back home.

As I sat in the small and crowded coffee shop watching people order baguettes with three types of cheese, Haitham told me that the most important thing one needed to have in this place was the right contacts. It was the difference between getting the scoop — the exclusive — and getting beat. I quickly realised how competitive news-gathering was. Haitham also explained how the AP's office was in the Jerusalem Capital Studios building along with most of the other foreign press. CNN was on the second floor with us; Reuters and Fox were downstairs; a floor above was the BBC and Agence France Presse; further up were ABC America, ABC Australia, Sky, CBS and some European networks. It meant that everyone pretty much knew everyone else's business. Whenever a politician or talking head was visiting someone's office, the rest could always doorstop them as they came out. Breaking news was hard to keep secret, and it was usually a rush for the lifts to cover a story before everyone else did. Luckily for us, we didn't have as many stairs to descend in our haste to get out there.

My studio apartment was in Nachlaot, a conservative neighbourhood where many of the women wore scarves on their heads. Spoken English wasn't as pervasive as I'd been led to believe. I went to a nearby supermarket to buy some supplies. At the check-out I handed over a 200-shekel note to the cashier, who said something sharply to me in Hebrew and threw my money back in my face. Perhaps I felt the sting of that insult more because I'd just come from living in Asia, where people handed you money using both hands, but I didn't know why the cashier was rejecting it and no one seemed to want to help me. I stood there with my money in my hand and refused to make way for the person waiting in line behind me. Finally, another cashier came up to the counter and spoke to me.

'She doesn't have enough money to break your note,' she told me.

'That's it?' I asked as I pulled out a smaller note and handed it to the woman, who continued to rant at me in Hebrew even though I understood nothing.

I was so tired from all the travelling and jetlag had finally caught up with me so I just crashed when I eventually made it back to the studio.

⁓

Three days later, as the sun went down on my first Friday in Jerusalem, I heard singing coming from one of the houses in my neighbourhood. I turned down the television to listen and the harmonies permeated the door of my little flat. As I would discover, practically everything shut down from sunset Friday to sundown Saturday. It was a lesson I learned the hard way, when I ran out of supplies and found that all the shops were closed. There was a knock at my door. Alon, my landlady's son, invited me to *Shabbat* dinner with his family. Surprised but grateful, I accepted and went upstairs to their home.

I stood with Alon and his parents around the dinner table as Tzipi's husband lit candles and sang a prayer. Alon, wearing a white satin skullcap on his head, sang along with his father but quickly pulled off the cap once the prayer was over. I watched as Tzipi shuffled in and out of the kitchen with different pots stacked on top of each other. Chicken was served first, followed by creamy vegetables. The plates were changed with each course. I'd never had a kosher dinner before, and it took a while before I realised that that was what was being served. I knew something about kosher food, how certain foods were cooked separately, but this was the first time I'd got to experience it. Dessert was fruit in a sickly sweet milk. I grimaced as I swallowed. I don't really have much of a sweet tooth, but I looked up at Tzipi and smiled.

It was very good of them to think of me and have me in their home. Since Alon had been to Australia, Sydney in particular, we had something to talk about, which was nice. Their English wasn't great and my Hebrew was non-existent, so Alon spent much of the night translating, explaining each dish. He told his parents and me in turn about his travels in Sydney and the different landmarks he remembered, how he sold tie-dyed T-shirts down by Sydney Harbour and used the money to finance the next leg of his trip. It was a change for me to be in a family atmosphere after having lived far from home for a while.

The next day I was scheduled to do my first real story—a feature on Israelis travelling to the West Bank, to the town of Nablus, on Saturdays, to take advantage of the cheaper prices and the luxury of doing something on the Sabbath, or

Shabbat as they called it. I was nervous about the assignment and how I would fare, but tonight I concentrated on my new surroundings. I listened to neighbours sing for the Sabbath and marvelled at the contradictions of the Israeli people I'd met so far. I'd been interrogated and screamed at and I'd been welcomed and fed. I realised it wasn't going to be easy to figure this place out, and I didn't have the faintest clue where to start.

CHAPTER TWO

Saturday 23 September 2000

On Saturday morning I set off for Nablus with Ibrahim and Elizabeth Dalziel, an AP photographer who'd arrived from Mexico months before I turned up. Elizabeth was five years older than me, had a short black bob and a petite frame that belied her enormous voice. I'd first met her two days before when we'd gone to lunch with two other photographers in the office. When the waitress came to take our order Elizabeth stretched back in her chair and said very loudly, 'I'm on a diet so can I get a steak?' I liked her immediately.

Nablus was bright and hot. We hooked up with APTN cameraman Abed Khabisa at Tappuah Junction and he drove ahead of us into Mas'ha village. The main road—the only road, actually—had been turned into an open-air market where shopkeepers displayed their wares right on the street. There was no footpath; people tripped over ceramic pots, stacks of carpet, running shoes and Levis jeans. I stiffened at one point when I saw two armed border police walking among the crowd. I was not accustomed to seeing people with guns. It would only take days for it to become a typical sight for me.

Ibrahim and I went into a furniture warehouse as Elizabeth and Abed went to take pictures. We watched as the Palestinian shopkeeper bargained furiously in Hebrew over the price of an item with an Israeli woman in jangling jewellery and heavy make-up. It sounded as if they were arguing but I was pretty confused because I didn't understand a word. It all seemed to work out because they shook hands and she walked off satisfied. I looked at Ibrahim, my face clearly screaming, *Help! Translation please!* He laughed and repeated the conversation: the woman wanted the furniture home delivered and they were discussing the day and time he could bring it over. Then we spoke to the owner and I breathed a sigh of relief when he began talking to us in Arabic.

Until then, I was worried my Lebanese Arabic would be completely different from Palestinian Arabic. I had had a lot of trouble deciphering much of Egyptian Arabic watching those soap operas, and hoped I wouldn't have this problem here. I ventured hesitantly a few words in Lebanese Arabic, the language I grew up hearing, but I knew my own tortured pronunciation of the words—complete with Australian accent—would take a while to improve. That was another reason why I wanted to be in the Middle East; I wanted my Arabic to get better. The teasing we'd experienced in Lebanon only made me more determined. I always hated that the Arabic language people spoke was different from classical Arabic, the written word. Classical Arabic would have made things so much easier when it came to reading, writing and speaking to all the people across the region. This was something that had annoyed me ever since my first Arabic lessons many years before.

Under the harsh sunlight we walked through the market and I took notes as I spoke to the Israeli shoppers and the Palestinians manning the different stalls. My editor wanted the piece as a harbinger preview of the thing the peace process would most embody—co-existence. What a wonderful thing it would be when the Palestinians and the Israelis got along so well. Indeed, some of the 'vox pops'—short question interviews with people on the spot—that we did for the TV camera suggested the Israelis didn't have a problem with coming out to the West Bank to shop. They enjoyed the experience and didn't seem to fear for their safety.

This was the sort of thing I was meant to be covering in the lead-up to the Palestinians declaring their state. I still didn't know what the hallmarks would be. I'd bought a ton of books on the Middle East from my favourite bookshop in Singapore and planned to read them all in advance, but time had run away from me and I arrived none the wiser about the history of the conflict. Years later, I still haven't read most of these books.

Several days later, Elizabeth and I went out to cover a protest in east Jerusalem by the Israeli peace group 'Peace Now'. They were outside the office of the Interior Ministry for Arab-Israelis, or Palestinians, queuing for Jerusalem ID cards. Palestinians carry identity cards in different colours: blue means you live in east Jerusalem, while orange indicates the West Bank (orange for after the Palestinian Authority was established and green for before) and Gaza cards were red before the PA, and green afterwards. They had to attend the office in order to register births, deaths and marriages, just like everyone else. I spoke to some women who'd been waiting at the office since early morning and was quite surprised by the way they had to do this—wait in line for hours in the hot sun outside the office, only being admitted inside a few at a time, up until noon each day—it was horrible. At the Interior Ministry for Israelis in west Jerusalem, everyone could go inside and sit down. There was also a cafeteria, where a little old man made sandwiches and poured hot coffee. That was where I went to get my work permit. The difference in the facilities was staggering. One woman at the Arab-Israeli office had four children and had only managed to register two so far.

'I can't come every day,' she told me. Another wanted to get her daughter's marriage registered, even though the wedding was months away.

After the protest we walked through the Old City. It was my first visit to that historic place and I tried to absorb every detail I could—the narrow, curving alleyways, the short arches, the names of all the different sites: the Via Dolorosa and the Seven Stations of the Cross. *Could this really have been where Christ stumbled while carrying the cross to his crucifixion? Up this narrow stairway that squeezes past a barber shop and a butcher?* My thoughts just tumbled.

We wandered through the winding corridors of the Arab section, doing our best to politely refuse the unending parade of hawkers beckoning us into their shops. We couldn't stop to inspect a tapestry or a rug without inviting more soliciting. We took a break in a little coffee shop and sat on little stools while we drank Arabic coffee served in little glasses. We watched the old men sitting near us, playing backgammon and cards, or smoking waterpipes and drinking tea. It was a lovely little corner, inside a cobblestone building, the age of which I couldn't begin to guess.

The market was in full swing as we came through the Damascus Gate. The names of different vegetables were flung into the air just like the oranges one man was tossing to another standing by a cart not too far away. At the top of the steps that led out we saw blue-and-white police cars, but they didn't look like normal Israeli police cars. We watched police-men leap out of the vehicles and run down the steps, only to be heckled by the vendors, shoppers and bystanders sitting along the steps watching all the activity. *Palestinians heckling Israeli police? And Israeli police ignoring all the insults? This could not be for real*, I thought.

When the police cars screeched up again and the police-men ran down the steps again in exactly the same way, we started asking people around us questions. Someone pointed to the rooftop above Damascus Gate and said the man wearing the Hassidic beard and peering from one of the windows was Jean Claude van Damme. He was being chased by the police; the police in their fake cruisers. They were filming a movie in the Old City. Elizabeth and I looked at each other and shrugged. *May as well take a look.*

We talked our way past the security guards and got to the top of Damascus Gate and watched as the actor ran through some action scenes over and over. Watching him was exhausting.

'Hit me! Hit me!' van Damme said to one of the stunt men, banging his chest as he did so. We found out from one of his assistants that he was filming a movie called *The Quest*. Parts of it were being shot here and in Tel Aviv, as well as other places in the Middle East. We watched for a while, hoping to get a quote or two from him about what it was like to film in the Old City, whether he was worried he might cop some criticism for dressing as an Hassidic Jew, but he was never available. In between takes the make-up people would rush up to him and dab at the sweat on his face and neck or he would rehearse lines and action sequences with other actors. He was darting to and fro, a bundle of energy. After an hour of waiting and nothing more than a severely sunburnt nose for my troubles, we left.

I look back now on those initial days in Jerusalem and it is painfully obvious to me just how naïve I was, how much of a beginner I must have seemed to the people I met. To me, this was a new professional opportunity; to them, it was an all-engulfing challenge in what was becoming an untenable life. This was a conflict born long before I arrived and it would endure long after I was gone. And I was supposed to make sense of it all for the rest of the world? To systematically interpret it and be the eyes and ears for people living in other parts of the globe? Journalism is a daunting enough endeavour when you know the story well, and I certainly didn't. I felt like an impostor, yet at the same time I knew I could process the barrage of data coming at me and, with time, become the expert I was already expected to be, just as I had with every other story I'd covered. The trouble was, I didn't have the luxury of time — I had to know it now.

CHAPTER THREE

Thursday 28 September 2000

a s I eased into my new life, I struggled to grasp the intricacies of that monster called the Middle East Peace Process. In August, Israeli Prime Minister Ehud Barak had returned from Camp David fuming because Palestinian leader Yasser Arafat had rejected the latest offer for a settlement, which Barak claimed had yielded most of Arab east Jerusalem as the Palestinian capital and made inroads on sticky issues such as refugees and borders. The Israelis said their concessions had been substantial, but Arafat said they weren't enough and refused them. Only years later did the real details behind the negotiations emerge. There was in fact fault on both sides. Barak went into the summit focusing on Jerusalem, he refused to yield control over borders and airspace. Israel's determination to hold on to West Bank settlements and offer the Palestinians some Israeli territory in return would have cut up the West Bank into three parts, divided by Israeli roads and settlements. But the Palestinians did not counter with any plans of their own, refused to budge on the refugee issue, and tried to play down the importance of the Temple Mount compound, or al-Haram al-Sharif, to Jews and their religion. US President Bill Clinton had hoped that this Camp David meeting would produce the same success that President Jimmy Carter's Camp David summit with Israeli Prime Minister Menachem Begin and Egyptian President Anwar Sadat had achieved: détente and withdrawal. In the 1979 agreement, Israel returned the Sinai to Egypt, first raising the possibility that this kind of deal—trading land for peace—was the way to finally put an end to the conflict.

Once the 2000 talks collapsed, however, Barak and Clinton openly blamed Arafat, accusing him of not wanting to make a deal. Barak, who'd put his prime ministership on the line by even talking about Jerusalem—something even those in his Labor Party denounced—was desperately trying to defend himself against growing criticism inside his own country. I would learn that the basis of the agreement proposed between Israel and the Palestinians consisted of four major points. One was the issue of sovereignty of Jerusalem, particularly the Arab east that the Palestinians claimed as their future capital. Another was the plight of Palestinians, who became refugees after two wars, and their descendants, now numbering four million. The borders and territorial continuity were the third and fourth points. Most Israelis were shocked that Barak raised the prospect of dividing Jerusalem during the Camp David talks, and they were even more shocked when the offer was rejected.

Meanwhile, a battle was playing out among the hardliners. Benjamin Netanyahu and his old foe, right-wing politician Ariel Sharon, were squaring off in the lead-up to the vote for the top job in their conservative Likud Party. I'll never forget the disdain with which Sharon was dismissed then. He was a political pariah who seemed to be in the dusk of his political career. He was an old soldier who had quit his post as Defence Minister in disgrace in 1983 after he was found to be indirectly responsible for the carnage of Sabra and Shatila because he'd 'disregarded the danger of acts of vengeance', the Kahane Commission said at the time. The Phalange, a Lebanese militia had raided these two Palestinian refugee camps on the southern outskirts of (west) Beirut city and had slaughtered women and children, apparently in retaliation for the assassination of Lebanese Prime Minister-elect Bashir Gemayel. At least 800 civilians were killed. This was done with the support and assistance of the Israeli army, which then controlled the camp. Israeli tanks and soldiers surrounded the camp and yet the Lebanese militia were allowed in, even though it was clear they intended to avenge Gemayel's death.

The power struggle between Netanyahu and Sharon seemed to be coming to a head. Sharon planned to visit Jerusalem's Old City, in particular the holy site the Muslims call al-Haram al-Sharif, the Noble Sanctuary; what the Jews call the Temple Mount. Sharon said he intended to make the point that Jews should be able to pray wherever they wanted, including the compound housing the Dome of the Rock mosque and the al-Aqsa mosque — the third holiest site in Islam. But Sharon intended to make a spectacle of his visit. Palestinian officials said later that they'd warned Barak that it would turn ugly, that it would only be provocative, and that he should prevent Sharon from going. But Sharon did go — on 28 September 2000, with some 1500 police for extra security.

The day before, on the Wednesday, I was in the office planning the next day's events. I was to go to Tel Aviv to cover an internet industry exhibition, where the Palestinians had their own stalls for the first time. I remember my news editor Karin Laub saying that the next day was going to be a big *balagan* in Jerusalem.

'What does *balagan* mean?' I asked.

'It's Hebrew for "big mess", "lots of trouble",' Karin said. 'It could be the beginning of another *intifada* [uprising].'

Was she kidding? It seemed hardly possible, with all the talk of peace, that something like that could start up again.

I was in Tel Aviv on the Thursday with Lefteris Pitarakis, an AP photographer who'd arrived in Jerusalem from Athens several months before me. We toured the giant exhibition hall and saw the different Palestinian show stands. There was one from PalTel, a new telecommunications company, and one for a technology park slated for Erez on the border of Israel and the Gaza Strip. Suited-and-tied businessmen laughed and backslapped and schmoozed in Hebrew and Arabic. Many of them had driven to Tel Aviv from Gaza City and Ramallah. The car park was dotted with cars bearing green and white Palestinian plates.

Lefteris and I sat down and had ice cream and started talking. I couldn't believe he was my age, 25, and I insisted he showed me his passport. I was even more surprised to note he was actually only nine days younger than me; he always acted much older. While we took our break he rang a photographer in Jerusalem and then told me that it had been a big day in the Old City: riots and police and lots of scuffles. I didn't know what to make of it. This was a religious site, holy to more than one religion. I knew people fought over religious things—they had done so since the beginning of time—but I couldn't have guessed what would happen next.

⟋⟋⟋⟍⟍

Friday 29 September was supposed to be my day off and I was going to use it to go flat hunting. I had scouted different suburbs in west Jerusalem to find a place close to the office since I didn't have a car. I just wanted a small one-bedroom apartment in a nice neighbourhood that was close to shops, but I was finding that just getting around Jerusalem and learning its geography was enough of a challenge. In the afternoon I got a call from the office.

'Can you get to Mokassid Hospital in east Jerusalem? Five people have just been shot dead.'

'Sure,' I replied, while my mind screamed, *What? What happened? Riots, scuffles, dead people? Would I see them? What was I supposed to do?* I didn't even know where the hospital was.

I tried to hail a cab but driver after driver sped off once I told them where I wanted to go. There have been many stories told about Israeli taxi drivers and they're all true. Here, they—Jewish and Arab drivers—decided before you entered their vehicle whether your destination was amenable to them and they would charge you their own price, conveniently forgetting to check the meter. The rudeness of these taxi drivers wildly exceeded my expectations and fears. During my time in Jerusalem at least two of them managed to reduce me to tears after bickering over the fare. Today, I was getting nowhere. Then the office rang back, calling off my expedition. Nasser Shiyoukhi, our Hebron stringer, had got to the hospital and was already filing reports from there. I volunteered to come into the office anyway; it appeared to be an unusually busy day.

The newsroom was in pandemonium. Staff on the news desk were on the phones speaking with reporters in the West Bank and Gaza, who were calling in details. The photo department was busy editing pictures to send out. TV people were rushing around with tapes in their hands, hurrying to edit film, cut packages, answer phones and issue orders to cameramen in the field. I sat at a spare computer, logging on to read what had already been written and filed about the day's events. The reports continually changed with updates on the wounded, comments from various officials and sudden spurts of violence.

As a writer for the AP my stories were edited and filed, then they went out on the internet, to the computer screens of other news agencies and in newspapers and reports around the world. It wasn't unusual to watch CNN and see them quoting an AP report, a story we would have just sent out, together with photos and television footage and radio reports.

I heard Haitham take a call from a Palestinian TV cameraman in east Jerusalem. An angry Arab crowd had thrown rocks at him. Only his shouting at them in Arabic managed to make them stop. Karin wanted more details from the hospital and asked me to head there to meet up with Nasser. There was a bit of uncertainty about safety; people in the office didn't know what kind of situation I would be walking into. Apparently the scene around the hospital was turning violent. I was nervous. Someone gave me a motorbike helmet to wear for protection. Tentatively, I took it. It was too big and I was too embarrassed to put it on.

After several tries, I managed to find a taxi driver who said he would take me most of the way to Mokassid but he wanted 50 shekels for the ride, at least double the standard fare. I didn't have much choice so I accepted. He dropped me off more than two blocks away from the hospital. I walked along the road as it curved along a hilltop overlooking Jerusalem and came upon a group of teenagers loitering. I stopped to see what they were doing. In the middle of the road, they'd set tyres alight. Several border police stood at the corner of the road watching them. The street was littered with jagged stones. I put my head down and continued walking, stopping occasionally to ask directions, still holding the helmet firmly.

Finally I turned into the main entrance of the hospital, where men standing out the front eyed me warily. I cringed inside, anxious, scanning the unfamiliar faces. Thankfully Nasser appeared and greeted me, and we entered the hospital. We squeezed past men and women crowding the stairways and corridors and pushed our way to the emergency wards. I saw male nurses gesticulating wildly outside operating theatres. They tried to push back screaming relatives, who were surging against the doors. I nearly tripped over women in black scarves, who were crammed into corners and just sat, crying and raising their hands into the air in despair. People jostled each other out of the way to read the lists of the injured posted outside the hospital doors. Everywhere I looked in the emergency room I saw people on stretchers. We stood to one side to observe the scene and tried not to interfere with the doctors' work. Others weren't so reticent, reaching for the doctors and tugging at their white coats for answers. One man, bald and sweating furiously, grabbed a doctor and pleaded.

'Please, help my son, my son. God protect you, my son,' the man said. The doctor held him firmly by the shoulders and spoke to him.

'Pull yourself together. Rely on God, rely on God.'

Moments later, we heard that his son was declared brain dead; shortly after, the old man himself was brought into emergency on a stretcher. He'd collapsed upon hearing the news.

I hate hospitals. I hate everything about them. The smell, the squeaky sound shoes make on the mopped floors, the white coats, the stethoscopes, the smell of sick people who haven't been out of their beds in ages. The memory of when my grandmother was dying in Beirut hits me every time I enter a hospital. I was fourteen and my sisters and I were shuffled in to see her and say our goodbyes. She had wasted away and didn't recognise us. We were grossed out when one of our aunts walked back into the room with a bedpan she'd just emptied. We just wanted to get out of there. We didn't know how to deal with the situation. In unguarded moments I always remember that time. If I'm in a hospital and get a whiff of disinfectant I need to struggle to repress the nausea that comes over me.

The doctors at Mokassid were overwhelmed. The shock of what had happened, the rioting at the compound following Sharon's visit, overwhelmed both the Israelis and the Palestinians. Throughout Israel, the West Bank and Gaza people reacted differently. In the Palestinian areas people took to the streets, demonstrating against Sharon and what they saw as his attempt to control an Islamic holy site. Elsewhere, people were praying and fighting. In Jerusalem's Old City, where the religious places are so close together, the praying increased the tension as the worshippers congregated at their holy sites at the same time. From the Haram al-Sharif Muslims looked down onto the Western Wall, known as the Wailing Wall, where the Jews came to pray. They threw shoes at them—a major insult in the Arab culture—thus disrespecting the Jewish sacred site and rituals. The Israeli police then stormed the Muslim compound, firing tear gas and beating protesters, violating their religious space.

The Palestinians in the West Bank and Gaza Strip turned their anger to the most obvious and convenient target: the Israeli army checkpoints. Demonstrators marched to their nearest checkpoint and took out their frustration on the soldiers, hurling rocks and Molotov cocktails. The Israeli response that day was too harsh and disproportionate—they fired on the protestors with rubber-coated steel pellets and tear gas. The ferocity of the attacks resulted in the death of six people and fuelled the Palestinian retaliation that was to last for days and weeks and months and years. Perhaps the army should have used the same crowd control methods they use on the Israelis when they riot—rubber bullets and batons—but they didn't. The result was fatal.

❧

Karin called me the next day and asked me to go to Gaza to help with the coverage there. She said I should pack some clothes in case I didn't return to Jerusalem that day. I didn't have a chance to tell my landlady I might be away for a few days. I should have found another place by now, but hadn't. I took a small red suitcase with me, packed with enough clothes for a few days away, and left the rest of my things in the studio. I needed to learn how to travel light, a practice that I was still trying to fine-tune. As I walked to the office, trailing my little red suitcase behind me, my parents called me on my mobile phone, frantic.

'What's going on over there? It doesn't look good, *habibi*,' my father said, using the Arabic word for 'sweetheart'.

'I don't know Dad, I just got here,' I said, before adding excitedly, 'I'm going to Gaza today.' I couldn't disguise my excitement; I'd never been to Gaza before and I was psyched by the prospect.

'Is that any safer? We're watching it here on TV. Please be careful, okay?' he said. I told him I was fine.

When I walked into the office Karin met me at the door.

'Oh Jamie, we've sent someone else to Gaza, but can you go to Ramallah? There's a funeral there we'd like you to cover.'

'Oh, okay,' I answered, disappointed, but still anxious to get out into the field.

∽

Elizabeth drove us to Ramallah in her car, a journey that took only about 20 minutes. Later, when all the checkpoints and roadblocks were set up, travelling to the town would take the better part of an hour. We arrived in Ramallah just before noon prayers were to get underway and the funeral was to begin. We loitered for a while, speaking to other photographers who had also come to cover the funeral. Slowly the crowd began to build and the area outside the main mosque filled with cars and people carrying Palestinian flags and wearing *keffiyehs* (black and white chequered head scarves).

I scribbled in my notebook everything I was seeing and momentarily lost Elizabeth. Then I spotted her on top of a building opposite the mosque, a good vantage point. I climbed the stairs to the roof and joined her. I watched as protesters burned an Israeli flag and stomped the flames out with their feet. Again, the use of the shoes—more insults. Elizabeth and the other photographers started snapping away when the mourners brought out the body, wrapped in a Palestinian flag. They carried it shoulder high on a stretcher.

I leant over to take a good long look. He seemed a bit pale, I thought. Strangely I didn't feel sadness, or disgust. I just wondered about the corpse being carried around in the sun all day; it was going to smell. I stood back as the photographers took pictures. I watched as the mourners proceeded through the twisting streets of downtown Ramallah before they crammed into their cars to drive to the hills where the hometown of the man who'd died was. We followed.

Up in the hills our mobile phone signals kept cutting in and out. Finally Karin, who'd been trying to reach me for ages, got in touch and asked me to head to Nablus that same afternoon.

'They're going to bury the governor's son today,' she said. He'd been killed during clashes in Nablus. I had no idea how I was going to get there or who would take me. By some bizarre stroke of fortune an orange minicab was part of the crowd surging towards the cemetery. I climbed past the throng and shoved my head in the window.

'Can you get me to Nablus?'

The driver nodded. 'Sure, let's go.'

It was a bumpy ride. Most of the main roads were blocked off and burning tyres or other debris littered the way. To avoid Israeli army checkpoints, the driver turned off the road and we crossed over rocks and dirt.

'This way, we won't get delayed,' he said to me, as I clung tightly onto the door handle while the van shook and rattled. When we reached the outskirts of Nablus I called Mohammed Daraghmeh, our stringer based in Nablus, to see where he was so we could meet up. He told me to come to Joseph's Tomb, where the demonstrators were and he would see me there. I could hear shooting in the background as he spoke. In my head I was thinking of the Nablus from my assignment at Mas'ha village only a week earlier and trying hard to imagine what I would now find. I tensed up as I listened to Mohammed, his voice calm despite the obvious danger.

'I am here, at the clashes,' he said. 'Just come, the driver will know where to bring you.' He sounded remarkably nonchalant considering where he was, but by then I'd noticed that most Palestinians seemed to be relaxed around gunfire. Maybe it comes from the tradition that some have of firing shots in the air during weddings. Mohammed may have been calm but I wasn't at all. His seeming indifference only made me more nervous.

༶

On that Saturday, 30 September, Jamal al Dura and his twelve-year-old son Mohammed walked into the middle of a confrontation between Palestinian gunmen and Israeli soldiers near the Jewish settlement of Netzarim in the central Gaza Strip. Seeking cover behind a wall, Jamal tried to shield his son from the flying bullets, screaming for the shooting to stop. More bullets flew. There was more screaming, and then Mohammed's body slumped against his father's, dead. Moments later Jamal also keeled over, shot and gravely injured.

The entire incident was captured by a television camera and beamed around the world. Many blamed the Israelis for killing a boy in cold blood. The footage also became a rallying cry for Palestinians to continue to fight against Israel. Mohammed al Dura became an icon of the Palestinian struggle. His picture was used afterwards in many propaganda films to prop up support whenever the struggle wavered. His image featured in patriotic music videos, calling on other children to follow him to paradise. But wherever paradise was, one thing was becoming abundantly clear to me: it certainly wasn't here.

CHAPTER FOUR

30 September–10 October 2000

It was like a blockbuster with surround sound. The gunfire that greeted me when I arrived in Nablus that afternoon evoked one of those mad shooting scenes where the actors never run out of bullets. The driver stopped at the top of the hill that led down to Joseph's Tomb.

'You sure you want to get out here?' he asked me. I looked back at him wide-eyed.

'It's not like I have a choice,' I said. His bottom lip jutted out as he put the van into park. I climbed out and looked around. There were only men on the streets and they eyed me suspiciously. I hated this. The driver pointed to a steep road leading to the Tomb. I paid him and made my way towards it.

'God be with you,' he said before driving off.

'Oh, great,' I said back in English, more to myself since he didn't understand a word I said.

My entire body was shaking as I stumbled down the hill, and my heart beat wildly against my rib cage. I felt completely unprepared and unprotected.

Joseph's Tomb is a small stone building with a sarcophagus made of marble. Jews believe it holds the remains of their patriarch, Joseph, of the technicolour dreamcoat fame. Muslims say an old sheik was buried there and his name, too, was Joseph. It's Area C surrounded by Area A—an Israeli-controlled Palestinian area inside a Palestinian-controlled Palestinian area. If that sounds confusing, it is.

Jewish students use the Tomb and the small building that houses it as a seminary. They go there to study the Torah, Jewish holy scripture, travelling on a bus in and out every day under Israeli army escort.

This was another site that was supposed to be a place of worship but had been turned into a place of violence. They were making war on holy ground and they wanted the world to side with them, not the 'other'.

I found Mohammed about 100 metres from the Tomb, where demonstrators were throwing rocks and Molotovs at the Israeli soldiers ensconced within the small outpost. At the end of the street the Red Crescent, the Muslim Red Cross, had taken over a building to set up an emergency medical clinic. Mohammed and I watched as men and boys, some as young as ten, went in to have their injuries tended before going back out again to throw more stones and flaming bottles filled with petrol. I tugged on the arm of one boy who said he was fourteen.

'Why are you going back out there?' I asked. He just shook off my question and pulled away from my light grip.

'We have to get them out of here,' he said, and walked off.

Suddenly, the soldiers inside the Tomb began firing heavily in our direction. We ran into the exposed ground floor of a building, which was still under construction, and waited for the shooting to abate. For about 30 minutes it didn't. We realised helicopters were also firing down on the protesters, as were soldiers at a hilltop position far above the town. They were now shooting from three different directions onto the one area. I stood and listened as the bullets fell like rain from the sky. *When will it end?*

Dusk fell, and Mohammed was keen to leave. He waited for a lull and urged me to go with him. I wasn't sure it was safe.

'Come on *'ammi*,' he called to me. *'Yalla.* Let's go.' Mohammed had called me 'uncle', a term of endearment, to show me that he considered himself to be like my uncle and therefore he would take care of me. It was a very Arab thing to do. He actually still calls me that, years later. *Yalla* means 'let's go' in Arabic.

I took a deep breath, shook my hair from its ponytail and swung by my side the stills camera I always carried with me as we made our way back up the hill. *This is crazy.* I was heart-stoppingly conscious of the soldiers on the hill, miles away, with their guns pointed at us, hoping against hope they could see through their sights that I was a girl carrying a camera and therefore they wouldn't shoot me. Luckily for me they didn't.

⤜∾⤛

Contrary to the information we had originally been given, we found out that the governor's son, Jihad Aloul, would be buried the following day. Mohammed invited me to his home while we worked out our schedule. There I met his wife, Mervat, a petite brunette with a husky voice. She laughed when I told her how much the cab fare to Nablus had been, telling me he'd ripped me off. She then invited me to stay for dinner.

As I sat down I looked at all the homemade food on the table.

'All this food reminds me of my mother's cooking,' I told her. I recalled my mother's cauliflowers, crispy golden brown and wrapped in Lebanese bread with a smattering of salt. So simple yet so delicious; something I was really craving at that point.

'She deep-fries them, right?' Mervat asked. I nodded. We talked about the similarities between Lebanese and Palestinian food.

'The only thing that's really different is the bread,' I said.

'Yes, the Lebanese bread is very thin. We have that here too, you know,' she said.

I nibbled from the different dishes and Mohammed worked the phones, answering the office's questions about what had happened that day. It was decided that I would spend the night there but as I had left my little red suitcase in the office in Jerusalem—I had expected to return there after covering the funeral in Ramallah with Elizabeth rather than end the day in Nablus—I didn't have a change of clothes with me. Mervat lent me some bright yellow pyjamas and I slept on a foam mattress on the floor of their living room, huddled under a thick blanket.

My eyes flashed open at dawn when a man started singing loudly outside the window. Before I launched into a volley of swearing at being awakened so early, I realised it was the muezzin making the Muslim call to prayer from the minaret of the mosque. I hadn't heard it at dawn before and I did try to get back to sleep afterwards but it wasn't going to be so easy. Closing my eyes, I heard whispers and peeked over my blanket to the door where Mohammed's three young sons, Ahmed, Alaa and Hisham, were standing, staring at me. I suppose seeing a girl asleep in yellow pyjamas on their living room floor was a bit of a surprise. Mervat had a surprise for me too; at breakfast she served fried cauliflowers. I was so happy I could have eaten the whole plate but I remembered my manners and refrained. The boys just watched me without saying too much. It must have been a confusing morning for them.

᠅

That Sunday morning it felt as if Nablus was a different place. There was a bustling open market in the middle of the town and vendors shouted their wares and prices while women of all ages balanced baskets filled with goods on their heads. Mohammed and I met up with TV cameraman Abed Khabisa and Nasser Ishtayeh, another AP photographer, for some good strong Arabic coffee. We all stood on a street corner and had one-shekel espressos, mixed with cardamom. I was beginning to develop a fondness for this; I loved the smell of the cardamom. They told me Lefteris would be joining us and that he would be bringing my suitcase.

'I guess this means I won't be leaving any time soon,' I said. I hadn't found an apartment yet and was now living out of my suitcase, which was dutifully following me around this strange place.

When Lefteris arrived I ran to greet him as he got out of the car. I gave him the biggest hug, regardless of local etiquette or stares. I was just so relieved to see him again.

'Hey, are you okay?' he asked me.

'Yeah, just happy to see you,' I said. I felt overwhelmed by what was happening. I'd been in the country for only ten days and it was all a bit much for me. One minute everything seemed peaceful and I was slowly getting used to the new job, the new environment, the new people; the next I was slipping, snatching at anything that resembled something familiar and logical. None of this was making any sense to me.

I was not used to gunmen, to seeing people go to their likely deaths or to feeling the anger that radiated from the funerals and processions. To watching boys flail about in clouds of black choking smoke from burning tyres, flinging whatever projectiles they had at hand, and then the sputters of gunfire and the screams. Seeing their limp bodies heaved back on the shoulders of their friends who cry out, 'Ambulance! Ambulance!' Watching as paramedics ducked bullets to collect them, piling them into the back of their ambulances that would then tear down the road, sirens blaring, to the nearest hospital. Knowing that mothers and fathers and whole families, who'd heard that their children were at the hospital, would have to rush to emergency, agitated and angry, grabbing at doctors, pulling back the green hospital curtains to see if it was their boys who'd been wounded; some would even have to go to the morgue to identify the bodies, stacked in metal drawers that slammed shut, the clang reverberating in the cold room.

From the beginning the Palestinians turned their private expressions of grief into public displays of outrage. Faces contorted, they carried flags and posters of the dead people they called 'martyrs'.

'With our souls and our blood, we'll redeem you, oh martyr,' they'd cry. I'd heard similar chants before, in Lebanon, during the war. But the cries there had been for those who were still alive—Michel Aoun or Samir Geagea, perhaps—not for someone who'd died. This was angry and vengeful, not motivating and supportive. I remembered the rallies in Lebanon as festive, people had turned the demonstrations into excuses to party and hang out with friends. The difference could not have been more marked for me than in the middle of this funeral where nary a smiling face was seen.

I felt very weird whenever Mohammed and I walked to the medical outpost to check with the doctors about the wounded and Mohammed would ask, 'Are there any martyrs today?' That word had a completely different meaning for me, coming from my Catholic schoolgirl background. It meant someone who was persecuted because of their faith — not someone who went out on the streets to die. I thought of St Jude boiling in hot oil, or St Peter being crucified upside down. These were the people I was taught were martyrs. The idea of someone who fought and was killed being made a martyr made no sense to me. I couldn't ask the question in the same way when I spoke to the doctors. It was always, 'Has anyone died today?'

I noticed an immediate cottage industry of poster makers. Miraculously, posters featuring a dead person's face against a backdrop of the Dome of the Rock appeared without fail on the morning of that person's funeral, pasted on walls and carried along with the body, which was wrapped in a Palestinian flag. Everything, everyone, became an icon. In death, they were lifted to heights many never saw, or even got the chance to aspire to, in life. The dead were glorified as heroes and Israelis were the enemy. Young men and boys were dying so quickly in the conflict's early days that the Israeli side accused Palestinian mothers of sending their children to the front line to perish — a charge the Palestinians denied.

The funeral we were covering that day was significant in its turnout, coupled with the fact that Jihad Aloul's father was the governor of Nablus, a highly respected man who felt the loss keenly. As mourners slowly made their way up the winding streets of Nablus to the cemetery at its hilltops, I tried to stay away from the men who marched at the front of the procession. They carried the body on a stretcher balanced on their shoulders and chanted and shouted and fired bullets in the air. It was hot and I was stuck in the middle of thousands of people. I could feel claustrophobia kicking in. The women followed, a sea of black and white headscarves, chanting furious slogans of their own. Palestinian police rode ahead of the procession, their trucks bearing floral wreaths. They too let off their automatic rifles, pointing the barrels up to the sky.

As everyone walked into the cemetery I ran into Nasser and told him I wanted to talk to some of the people inside the grounds. I knew that on my own I would put a few people off, so I would try to have a male colleague with me whenever I could. I was aware that my presence was unusual to the locals and that I was very noticeable—a Western woman with an uncovered head walking the streets yet speaking Arabic when talking to someone. Nasser stood by me as I approached a group of young men sitting on marble headstones, smoking and chatting among themselves. I couldn't really articulate my questions to the men because I was so unnerved by the constant gunfire. It sounded too close. I jumped every time a shot was fired but they tried to reassure me it was alright.

'Don't worry, don't be afraid. They're shooting in a different direction,' one of the men said with a wave of his hand, seeming to fail to grasp the logic of gravity—whatever went up had to come down.

'I just don't know why they're doing that,' I said. Another man lifted his head, inhaled his cigarette deeply and replied, 'They're getting their anger out. It's their way of expressing themselves.'

'Well I don't see the point,' I insisted. One of the men jumped up from his seat and reached into the back of his jeans. He pulled out a small handgun and started firing it into the air, just a metre in front of me. I was so shocked that I burst into tears. The others began chiding him: 'No, no, don't,' but by then I'd walked away, shaking. Nasser scolded them, 'See? You've upset her,' then he followed me.

While we stayed in Nablus, Lefteris and I would check into Al Qasr, the Palace Hotel, every evening, then every morning we would check out. Lefteris' reasoning was that we could be called away at any moment and wouldn't want to be delayed by the nuisance of packing and clearing out of a hotel when we needed to rush off. It was a wise strategy that later came in handy.

When we came back to the hotel at the end of each day I'd run a bath and just soak, letting the day slide off me. I'd then go next door to Lefteris' room and use his computer because I hadn't yet been assigned my own laptop. I'd check the wire to see what stories we'd put out, send some notes, quotes or details for the main story, and check my email. My inbox was filled with messages from friends who only weeks earlier I'd farewelled back home. They couldn't believe what was going on. Some of my journalist friends said they were envious. 'Timing is everything,' one wrote, while another stated something that I was thinking about but doing my best not to: 'Your parents must be having kittens!'

I was happy to hear from them. I felt far removed from my comfort zone and it was good to know they were thinking of me. I wrote back and told them how anxious I was about keeping safe. To add to my growing sense of rootlessness, our office manager in Jerusalem rang to tell me she'd cleared my stuff out of the studio I had been staying in because the landlady needed it for the next tenant. My things were in the office, waiting for me to get back. I really was homeless now.

Being Greek, Lefteris always insisted on a full dinner at night, regardless of the fact that most of Nablus was on a general commercial strike and many of the restaurants were closed. He would point out a coffee lounge for men only and joke, 'See, I should leave you behind and go and eat with the rest of the men.' Each time we drove past the closed local ice cream bar I would wistfully point it out, wishing I could feed on my most favourite thing of all.

I'd often have to translate for Lefteris as he didn't speak any Arabic. I'd laugh when he insisted on going alone into a store, knowing there would be problems. One day he ducked into a little shop to buy drinks and emerged moments later calling out to me, 'Jamie, please, come and see what she wants,' pointing to a little girl who then held out her hand to me.

'I just want to give him his change,' she said when I asked.

We would hit different take-away stands, having shawarma—lamb pressed and roasted on an enormous skewer and served in little pockets of pita-like bread peppered with salad, hummus and a good dollop of chilli. Our car, emblazoned with the letters 'TV', was easily recognisable to all the locals, so after a few days we became part of the local scene.

We heard three Israeli soldiers had been kidnapped on the border with Lebanon by Hezbollah guerrillas. The office rang to tell me I might have to head to the frontier to report on the scene. It intrigued me that they expected me to get from one end of the country to the other without a car of my own—not to mention that I was still without an apartment and living out of my little red suitcase. What surprised me even more was that I generally did manage to do so. In this instance, another reporter was sent from Jerusalem and I remained in Nablus.

Asked to do a story on Palestinian gunmen, Mohammed and I went to interview members of the Tanzim, the military wing of the Fatah movement, which Yasser Arafat headed. We managed to speak to three as they leant on a car, chatting. As we interviewed them on a main, open street in Nablus, cars would honk as they drove by and the men acknowledged them with waves. One car screeched up to inquire about bullets, which were being sold for one shekel (25 US cents) apiece. The men themselves were kitted out with automatic rifles and even had bulletproof vests. Two refused to give me their names; the one that seemed to be the leader, a man with short curly hair, asked to be called Tarek.

He said he knew how dangerous their activities were. He was married with children and while we were speaking his wife called his mobile.

'She just wanted to see if I had anything to eat. I left the house without breakfast,' he said.

Lefteris couldn't come with us—he was photographing stone-throwers and gunmen at Joseph's Tomb and when I saw his pictures later it was obvious he'd often been in the line of fire—but he told me to take a picture of the gunmen. I wasn't particularly confident in my skills and I also had to convince the gunmen to let me photograph them. Tarek refused but one of the others went off and returned soon with black material hoods. He cut out the eyes and put them over the head of his friend and himself. I took the picture and then Mohammed took the camera from me.

'Go, let me get one of you with them,' he said. *Was this going to be my first action shot?* Lots of reporters and photographers had pictures taken of themselves with rebels and soldiers to show that they'd met the people they wrote about. I guess that's why I agreed to do it; to prove I'd actually spoken to them.

During our time in Nablus we got to know the town and its surrounding villages. Nasser and his cousin Jaafar lived in the village of Salim, not far from Nablus. One day there was a funeral for one of Salim's youths and as we followed the procession that took place after the burial it became clear that clashes would break out. The Palestinian demonstrators were moving closer and closer towards an Israeli army roadblock. They had rolled burning tyres into the middle of the main road and, with the fierce sun beating down on us, it felt like we were walking into an inferno.

Lefteris continued to take pictures while Mohammed and I decided to try to get a better view from one of the hilltops. We drove higher and higher as the road wound up one hill. When we came near the top a few locals warned us there were Israeli soldiers nearby. We came out on top of the hill and I was impatient to get closer to where the riots would be taking place, so I could see what was happening. Suddenly Mohammed stopped the car.

'Why have you stopped?' I asked.

'Because there's army there, uncle,' he said, pointing in front of him. All I could see was an empty road and a brick wall along one side of a field.

'I can't see anything,' I said. He pointed again.

'Look, look,' he said. I sat back in horror. Some fifty metres away, a soldier in full camouflage gear stood up and pointed his gun at us. I raised my hands with my palms facing him and Mohammed did the same. The man motioned for us to stop the car and for me to come forward. Mohammed cut the ignition and I got out of the car and, with my hands still up, walked slowly towards him. It was only when I got closer that I saw a row of about eight soldiers with netting over their helmets and their rifles pointed at me. I swallowed deeply. I couldn't believe I hadn't spotted them.

I spoke as loudly and as calmly as I could: 'I'm a journalist —don't shoot.'

Eventually I got close enough to talk to them with ease, which was one of the benefits of being a woman; a man might not have been trusted to approach so near.

'You have to go back,' the soldier who seemed to be in charge said in his heavily accented English.

'I just wanted to see what the clashes were like from up here,' I explained.

'No, you have to go. They're shooting at us. If you stand here and talk to us, they'll shoot at you too.'

As if on cue, a shot rang past us and the soldiers scrambled back into their positions.

'Go back now!' the soldier shouted. I didn't need to be told again.

The level of the clashes was changing quickly, from boys with stones, to boys with petrol bombs and Molotov cocktails, to men with guns, to organised militias. They were taking over and creating a volatile battleground.

❧

One morning in Nablus, a couple of hundred masked Palestinian gunmen took to the streets in a show of force. They were marching in the centre of town to make the point that they were a proper militia, not the disorganised bands of men with guns the Palestinian Authority (PA) was dismissing them as. The PA at the time was trying to convince the world that the gunmen taking part in the daily clashes were gang

members, while the Israelis insisted they were members of
the Palestinian police force. However they looked, these men
wanted to be taken seriously by everyone. Lefteris ran to get
into the middle of the marchers to take pictures. I tried to
keep up but was at a loss: If I walked behind the men, I would
get lost in the fray. If I walked beside them, the crowds on the
sidelines would get in the way. Lefteris noticed my dilemma
and grabbed me, placing me in between the two columns of
masked men toting AK47s and M16s. As they marched on
either side of me I looked around to see if there was anyone I
could get a comment from. I turned to the front of the march
and saw a Jeep leading the men. I went up to one man
walking alongside the car and shouted into his ear: 'I need to
speak to whoever's in charge.'

The Jeep stopped briefly and two masked men pulled me
inside. A man screaming into a loudspeaker was sitting in the
front passenger seat. He had nearly lost his voice but turned
around and spoke hoarsely to me through a black ski mask
pulled over his face.

'We've got 400 armed men ready to fight Israel. We're
fighting them every day to free the Tomb,' he said to me. I
took down some quotes—all anonymous of course—and then
jumped out of the car as it slowly inched its way up the road.

Lefteris came running towards me, looking worried.

'I was looking for you,' he said. Later he explained that, as
he stood there taking pictures of armed men on his left and
his right, he heard some voices calling out my name.

'They were looking at me and calling "Jamie, Jamie", and
when I look for Jamie she's not here.' He spotted me
only when I jumped out of the Jeep. I knew I was starting to
get recognised around Nablus but his words discomfited
me somewhat. I didn't know if this meant I should curb my
brash behaviour—walking up to people, talking to gunmen

in broad daylight, jumping into a Jeep commandeered by masked men. After filing reports over the phone we took a break at a sweet shop. It was an interlude that only served to compound my sense of confusion.

～～⁓

We were lucky that evening to find the sweet shop named 'Arafat Sweets'—no relation to Yasser Arafat—in the suburb of Rafidia open for customers. For as long as I'd been in Nablus, everyone I'd met had sung the praises of this place, allegedly home to the best kanafe in the Palestinian areas. Kanafe is made from semolina wheat and drenched in a rich syrup. It's a speciality in the Middle East and I wanted to try it to see how it compared with the kanafe I'd eaten in Beirut, where you can get it in a little pocket of toasted bread with lots of syrup and sometimes even cheese. It was a great treat in the morning with tea or coffee. As we sat outside and dug into the dessert together with our requisite overpowering Arabic coffee, one of the attendants came up to our table and stood over Lefteris.

'You took my picture today,' he said. Lefteris looked at me, wanting a translation.

'He says you took his picture,' I replied. I shifted in my seat, hoping this wasn't going to lead to a confrontation. There were always some people in the mass of usually media-friendly demonstrators who didn't like to be photographed. They believed it could help Israeli authorities identify them and track them down. Lefteris put his cup of coffee down on the table.

'Okay,' he said. 'Tell him to wait.' He then ran to the car and returned with his laptop. He opened his photo files of the march and invited the man to sit down. Eventually our visitor was able to pick himself out of the crowd, swathed in a keffiyeh.

'There I am,' he said, pointing at the screen. We looked at him and smiled. He was completely masked and therefore unidentifiable. He went inside and returned with more coffee. After that, whenever we returned to Nablus we made a point of stopping there to say hello and get more kanafe. In fact, it was an unspoken rule in the AP office in Jerusalem that anyone returning from any assignment in Nablus had to bring back kanafe for everyone else in the bureau.

⤙⤚

It took about a week before a flak jacket (bulletproof vest) the office had ordered for me arrived. APTN's Abed Khabisa was able to bring one with him. It had been a complicated procedure getting it from the bureau and bringing it into the West Bank. By now, there were many roadblocks and checkpoints, making the journey for ordinary Palestinians cumbersome and time-consuming. We met Abed at a junction at the entrance to Nablus. Lefteris walked around to the back of the car and opened the boot, lifting out the white vest and handing it to me.

It's heavy, I thought as I tried to carry it with one hand. It weighed about twelve kilograms. Lefteris already had a grey one and he had made me wear it on previous occasions, when we went to the Tomb for example. It used to annoy me because he needed it more than I did—I wasn't in among the gunmen during the clashes, he was.

I now also felt bad that I had a jacket as none had arrived for Mohammed or Nasser Ishtayeh. Nasser wore a ridiculous orange fluorescent vest with 'PRESS' marked on it when he photographed clashes, as if that would protect him. I didn't like to wear my jacket when I went out with either of them. I wondered: *Why am I more special than them? They are the ones with the families. I am young and single.* It really bothered me. I couldn't shake this awful feeling that they might be considered more expendable than me because they weren't full-time staff. The AP obviously felt great responsibility towards me—I was specifically brought out to do this job. But I felt that being single, young and independent should have made me more expendable than them. I had my family in Australia waiting for me but I wasn't married and I had no children. I didn't have a boyfriend. There wasn't anyone cooking dinner for me at home waiting for me to return.

❧

At 7 a.m. on the morning of Saturday 7 October 2000, Lefteris beeped me on my walkie-talkie phone.

'Let's go—the Israelis have withdrawn from the Tomb.'

'What?' I shouted, suddenly wide awake. I bolted to get dressed and out the door. That was the only day we didn't check out of the hotel in the morning as we'd always done.

I knew that one soldier had died on the first day of battle at the Tomb. Shooting from Palestinian gunmen had prevented a helicopter from rescuing a wounded soldier and he subsequently bled to death. But this was the first time Israel was ceding territory in this young conflict. Everywhere else the military had boosted its presence.

We raced to the Tomb and found Palestinian police surrounding it. I was now very curious about this small space that had caused so much anger and death but we were not allowed to approach. Instead, I spoke to several people who lived in the area, including 62-year-old Abdul Fateh Sayed. He took me into his little bookstore, where dust covered most of the surfaces and shattered glass dotted the floor. Book after book had been shot through in the fire fights.

'Look here, here, here,' he said as a thick law book hit the desk with a thud, its centre clearly pierced by a single bullet that had nearly made it all the way through the leaves. He'd been unable to reach his shop while there was fighting at the Tomb but he and his shop were among the more fortunate. I visited one apartment building that also faced the Tomb. As I ascended the stairs, every step seemed to be covered with glass and bits chipped from walls. Some families invited me inside their bedrooms, where jackets and dresses were ripped by bullets while they hung inside wardrobes. Relatives who'd come to greet them, kissing three or four times on the cheeks, congratulated them on surviving and having something left of their home to salvage. I looked around, taking it all in.

'Come and see,' said one man, happy to show me the destruction. Bedroom mirrors were smashed and family portraits swung precariously from walls with the glass broken and the faces smeared with dirt. Living here had been too dangerous for most of them and they'd sought refuge with relatives who lived elsewhere. I wondered how they would piece their lives together after this, if it would be as hard as piecing together all those shattered frames and smudged pictures, and whether they would feel at peace even after everything was restored.

More and more people came to the Tomb. They were as curious as we were but also happy that the Israelis had left. Most, in fact, were jubilant. They'd won this battle, they told me; Palestinians in other towns would take heart from their experience and face the enemy more determinedly than before because they'd shown that it was possible to achieve an Israeli withdrawal. Men who'd rushed to the scene were shaking hands and kissing each other's cheeks, it seemed an eternity of kissing. The women began ululating, almost like yodelling, in that way that Arabs do when they're celebrating. But the jovial and relaxed atmosphere soon tensed up once the gunmen claiming victory arrived. They came standing in the back of pick-up trucks, many wearing masks and toting rifles.

These men ignored the lines of police and clambered to the top of the wall surrounding the enclave. They brought their flags of Palestine and Fatah and Hamas and they spoke with their megaphone of how they won the battle and how it was only the beginning, something many of the people there didn't appreciate. They'd been hoping that with the removal of the last remnant of Israeli presence in their town, they could get on with their lives. And here in front of them were trigger-happy men promising more violence. Some in the crowd cheered, which grew in number as more young men turned up. Something was about to give—it didn't take long.

The gunmen went from standing on the wall to standing on the dome that housed the Tomb. They stood on the Tomb and planted a Hamas flag and a Palestinian flag on its tip while others went inside and began throwing objects out the doors and windows. First it was the tents and boots the Israeli soldiers had left behind in their haste to evacuate, then it was the prayer books. Soon, black smoke began to billow from the tiny windows of the Tomb. Whistles and cheers soared from the crowd and others clambered onto the dome and started hammering into it, breaking through. Firefighters turned up to douse the flames on three separate occasions. Children started walking around wearing Israeli military vests and helmets which they'd found among the rubble.

At one point Lefteris came up to me and gave me his disk—he'd photographed some Palestinians standing on the sarcophagus and trashing the room.

'They're looking for me,' he said as I quickly slipped the disk into the pocket of my jeans. Sure enough, he was soon surrounded by Palestinian policemen. Since Lefteris couldn't speak Arabic, communication was difficult for both sides. I could see and hear them yelling at each other but I didn't want to approach because Lefteris had given me the disk so only he would be targeted and I wouldn't be harassed. So I called out to Mohammed and Nasser Ishtayeh, who managed to extricate Lefteris from what could have been a very messy situation.

Unable to endure my own raging curiosity any longer, I scaled the broken-down wall to go inside the enclave and have a look. The police didn't want me in there and told me it was still too dangerous. I ignored their advice and stepped gingerly over sopping sleeping bags and other discarded equipment and strewn bricks. As I approached the room with the Tomb inside I could feel the heat from the fire overpowering the atmosphere, keeping everyone back. I couldn't go far inside. The walls were black from the fire but saturated with water. The floor was flooded and the hollowed room was a symphony of dripping sounds and the hiss of steam.

'See,' said one man, pointing to an indentation in the side of one wall. 'This was a Muslim building. That points the direction to Mecca.' He felt that this sign, common in many Arab and Muslim homes and buildings for people wishing to pray, was enough to prove that Joseph had been a Muslim and not a Jew—therefore the Palestinians were entitled to lay claim to the site. I didn't know what to say. The marble sarcophagus itself looked relatively undamaged, if a little wet.

As I climbed over a crumbling wall I spotted Ahmed, a very cute, very young policeman. He was the nephew of a colleague who worked with Mohammed for a Palestinian paper. The first time I saw him, with a band of other policemen dressed in black arriving at the scene of clashes near Joseph's Tomb, I thought he looked too young to be carrying a gun. He couldn't have been 21. I smiled and said hello, then went to find Lefteris, who was sitting in our car. I noticed that we had a flat tyre.

Lefteris was using my black denim jacket to shield himself from the light to get a better view of his pictures. Children crowded all around the car, banging their hands on the windows and pointing, trying to get our attention. Lefteris' computer battery was running low. He swept out of the car, waving his arms and stamping his feet. Holding his laptop on his palm like a platter he lifted the electricity cable in his other hand and asked in English if there was somewhere he could get some power. Whether they spoke English was irrelevant, because a band of people put their arms around him and cheerfully gestured in the general direction of somewhere that had electricity. Off they went.

I got out of the car to take a closer look at our mobility problem. I knew how to change a flat tyre, but I also knew I wouldn't be able to do it here, with everyone watching me. I saw Ahmed standing nearby and noticed he was looking over at me. So I stood in front of the deflated tyre and kicked it a couple of times. That seemed to be enough. Blond and blue-eyed with an adorable smile, he came up and asked if I wanted him to change it and I silently opened the boot of the car. Enlisting the help of some younger boys, he quickly did the job. I had to content myself with pouring a bottle of water over Ahmed's hands so he could wash the grease off them.

When Lefteris came back, after having filed his pictures, I told him I was ready to leave. He reminded me that he first had to fix the tyre and I pointed out that it was already done.

With a raised eyebrow he looked at the tyre, then at me.

'I don't want to know how you did it, okay?'

I can only speculate as to whether the decision to withdraw from Joseph's Tomb was a serious error on Barak's part and contributed to his downfall later. The situation still appeared salvageable and the leaders were being flown to Paris and Sharm el Sheik in Egypt, beseeched by Clinton and French President Jacques Chirac to stop the maddening tennis game of action and reaction.

Back at the hotel, we learnt that a Jewish rabbi—an American no less, which was something that energised the US news organisations—had been killed; his body was found in a cave. Hillel Lieberman had come from the nearby Jewish settlement of Elon Moreh after mistakenly hearing that the Torah was being vandalised at the Tomb following the military withdrawal. Incensed, he set out to stop it. Instead, he was beaten to death, most likely by Palestinian militants, but this was never proven.

It was a bad time. Barak had issued a 48-hour deadline for all violence to cease. It was Yom Kippur, the holiest time on the Jewish calendar, and for a lot of Jews it recalled the Yom Kippur War of 1973, when Israel was attacked without warning by Egypt and Syria. I felt gloomy because everyone thought things would get much worse. The settlers were expected to go on a rampage once the sun went down, marking the end of Yom Kippur. Lefteris and I decided to stay inside as covering news at night was not the wisest move. If we weren't comfortable about a situation we wouldn't go through with it. This was something we'd decided from the beginning.

It was my tenth day in Nablus. I almost felt like I was starting to know what I was doing. Almost, but not quite.

CHAPTER FIVE

Wednesday 11 October 2000

W
e were sent to the Israeli settlement of Elon Moreh outside Nablus to cover Hillel Lieberman's funeral. Like many settlements, Elon Moreh was built on a wide and arid hill outside the main Palestinian town in that area. After I'd spent time in Gaza, I noticed that these settlements were built in certain spots, because of their proximity to water aquifers and because of the military advantage they offered. It was easier for the Israelis to control the Palestinian population if they had settlements surrounding their villages so they could block off the main roads to the areas.

Lefteris was wary of going because we'd spent so much time with the Palestinians and he didn't want them to turn on us if they found out we'd gone to a Jewish funeral. It could compromise our safety. He had a point. But since the Palestinians themselves couldn't make it to the outskirts of Elon Moreh, we figured it shouldn't be a problem. By now Israel had put restrictions on Palestinians travelling outside their towns, they needed special permits—work, medical—to move around. Even then, depending on the 'security' situation, Palestinians were often turned away at checkpoints.

It felt weird to leave Nablus, crossing the different checkpoints and leaving our colleagues behind. At one roadblock I recall a soldier looking at my passport and noting I was Australian. He squinted into the car and looked at me.

'You're from Australia? Don't you know there are Olympics in your country? What are you doing here?' It was a fair question. I'd watched the opening ceremony from a pub in Singapore but hadn't seen anything since. It was all over now, but I remembered wanting to be in Sydney when the Olympics were on. When I'd gone home to see my family the city was already buzzing with excitement about the coming Games, and now I had missed out. His question suddenly turned my thoughts to Sydney and its energy, the way it welcomed visitors and left them with a good impression of all things Australian. I thought of the beaches and the sunshine, my parents' backyard barbecues and my mother's cooking. I wanted to be there right then.

As our car wound up the hills of Elon Moreh we took a good look around. I'd never been inside a settlement before and I was surprised by what I saw. It was like going into a refugee camp and expecting everyone to be living in tents. They weren't, of course. Elon Moreh was suburbia: manicured lawns, footpaths and wide open streets with crossings, schools and shops. Everything seemed perfect. I later discovered most settlements looked like this. Even the houses had the same designs, the same brickwork, and the same colour.

The settlements and their occupants, some 250 000 people, were probably the sorest point in any peace plan proposals. Settlements in the West Bank and Gaza have grown more extensive under every Israeli administration, including those of Yitzhak Rabin and Shimon Peres, men who favoured the land-for-peace deal. For Palestinians there could be no greater provocation than to look across the valley and see a Jewish settlement growing ever larger. Built on Palestinian land, without permission or compensation, the settlements also often intersected Palestinian villages, cutting them off from each other and from 'by-pass' roads built for Israeli use alone. What Israel was doing was illegal according to international law, and yet each government carried on their expansion and turned a blind eye whenever settlers erected new outposts, even if the accommodation consisted of an errant ship container or a couple of tents. Over time the settlements would be assigned their own border police to protect them and secure the area. The Israeli government's money went into paving new and proper roads, extending electricity and communications to far-flung hilltops and employing more soldiers and border police to protect the communities.

Settlers themselves were either there for economic purposes—the land and the houses were cheap—or religious and nationalistic reasons. This was the Holy Land and God had granted them the right to be there. Many believed themselves pioneers; the first line of defence for those Israelis living cosy existences in the beachside cities of Tel Aviv and Haifa. But many of the Israelis I encountered in Jerusalem and Tel Aviv showed little empathy for the settlers.

Many people turned up for Lieberman's funeral. Some arrived from other settlements while others came in on buses from Jerusalem. The synagogue was packed and people spilled out to its grounds and onto the street. Lefteris donned a hat out of respect and went inside to take pictures of the body wrapped in a shroud and the male mourners. I went upstairs to where the women were. It had exactly the same sort of layout as a mosque—men downstairs, women upstairs and out of view. To me there were so many obvious similarities between the Muslims and the Jews. Religious men from both faiths covered their heads and grew beards. Religious women from both faiths covered their hair and wore modest clothing. Neither ate pork. And yet they were also so different.

After watching the prayers and seeing the people grieving I went outside to get some air. I ran into a BBC crew who'd arrived from Jerusalem to cover the funeral. They told me they'd heard rumours that the settlers weren't particularly friendly towards the press so they were keeping their distance. I looked around and saw some young men carrying automatic machine guns and wearing ripped shirts. I learnt later that torn clothing was a gesture of grief in Jewish tradition.

As the ceremony ended, the mourners planned to leave Elon Moreh in a procession of cars and buses and head to another settlement called Eli, where Lieberman would be buried. An army patrol would lead the convoy. I spoke to some people as they made their way to their vehicles. One man, a rabbi, pointed out the solemnity of the crowd and said even their grieving was done in a peaceful manner.

'Look at how calm everyone is,' he said to me. 'Does this look like a dangerous group of people?'

I had to agree. Around me people walked, their arms linked and their eyes rubbed raw. Sorrow, not anger, seemed to be the prevailing emotion, a stark contrast to the many Palestinian funerals I'd witnessed. People stood out of the way as the wife and daughter of the dead man stumbled along, weeping and clutching at each other. Girls watching the pair began to cry just upon seeing them.

Lefteris drove by and picked me up and we joined the convoy. As we left the entrance of the settlement and passed an Arab field, there was suddenly a commotion. Cars swerved to the side and pulled over and men carrying guns ran across the road and into the field, their side-locks swinging and ripped shirts fluttering in their wake. Some Palestinian children had thrown rocks at the procession and now the settlers were routing them out. The children were easily outnumbered and the settlers were armed. The children ran inside the one house in the middle of this field to escape the settlers. We watched as the border police stood by their Jeeps and observed the scene, making no move to stop anyone. The settlers ran to the house and began pelting it with rocks. We'd pulled over to the other side of the road, away from the field; Lefteris got out to take photos and was promptly stopped.

'Don't take any pictures if you want to keep your camera,' one man warned him in a New York accent, as clear as Central Park on a sunny day.

Two other male settlers lifted a giant rock and threw it through the back window of the BBC car, while another news car had its tyres slashed. Then we heard gunfire. That's when the border police decided to intervene. They forced people to continue on their way to the cemetery. But some stayed, huddling in ditches.

I got out of the car and crouched next to Lefteris. He couldn't take any pictures because a border police Jeep was blocking his line of sight. So he clambered quickly into the ditch behind us and ran a few metres down to get a better angle. Then the gunfire really spun out of control and I knelt down behind the car. I spotted Israeli soldiers shooting from about 30 metres behind us in the ditch, and helicopters started to fill the sky, firing down on what I assumed were Palestinian gunmen as I couldn't see. Soon the earth started to rumble and my body was lifted up and down from the ground over and over, landing me hard on my knees on the concrete. Then I saw the source of this seismic vibration turn the corner and I could scarcely believe my eyes. A tank. It was enormous, and I'd never seen one so close before.

It came nearer and nearer, the noise grew louder and louder and I struggled to pin myself to the ground as the reverberations picked me up and dropped me. It moved about 50 metres past where I was huddled and stopped. Then came another one, and there was more shaking and picking up and dropping. Now the gunfire was at its most intense and I could feel the wind from the bullets overhead as I ducked behind the car. I couldn't even reach into the boot to get my flak jacket. I realised how futile the protection of a hubcap was, but I couldn't slip into the ditch.

Lefteris looked over at me helplessly. I rang the office and yelled to make myself heard over the noise, telling them what was going on.

'Do you have some quotes to file?' someone asked. I hung up, I didn't have quotes to file, I just wanted them to know what was happening to me. This was almost what my life had boiled down to: spending the day in the field and ringing the office and giving them the details of what I was witnessing. I curled into the tightest ball I could and endured 45 minutes of unadulterated firepower, waiting for the bang bang to end.

Lefteris beeped me on the two-way once the shooting abated.

'Quick, come now,' he said. I raced over to the ditch, my heart in my throat. An Israeli camera crew was also crouched in there with him, and they were all joking and chatting to pass the time as bravely as they could. I smiled and pretended to be nonchalant, but I couldn't shake my discomfort, or my fear. *I'm not cut out for this.* I knew I couldn't sit there with bullets whizzing past me and dismiss it like they were doing. I didn't want to get comfortable. Not long afterwards the shooting died down completely and we were able to leave.

❧

Once we returned to Nablus, we met some of the men who had taken part in the gunfight. They were standing on the edge of one of the main streets of Nablus, watching boys run up and down looking for rocks they could fling at two Israeli Jeeps parked a couple of hundred metres away. The men's jeans were old and scuffed. They had short, dark curly hair and unshaven faces. They smoked—to me it seemed that all Palestinian men did, no matter their age. They stood and talked, seemingly well pleased with their efforts. They claimed it as a real victory—they were bringing the power of the Israeli military down to their guerrilla level of fighting. They were cocky and proud of their actions that day.

I stood there on the footpath and spoke to Karin on my mobile, relaying their comments. It eventually turned into one of the stories of the day. Without a laptop of my own I couldn't compose my stories; I relied heavily on everyone back in the office in Jerusalem to do it for me. They sent them to Lefteris' computer for me to read back and change as necessary. It was a frustrating way to work, but I was learning.

Lefteris' girlfriend Chryssa had come to Nablus before we got back and she was planning to stay a few days with Lefteris. The night we arrived back the three of us went out for dinner together with a girlfriend of Chryssa's. We dined at one of the restaurants that had reopened after the Tomb withdrawal, and ate really well. I envied Lefteris and Chryssa for the company they gave each other. Seeing the two of them laugh and hold hands and tease each other just made me feel even more alone. The phone calls that I had been receiving from friends in Singapore and Australia, while gratifying and heart-warming, weren't quite enough.

On 12 October 2000, Lefteris and I were in Tulkarem covering yet another funeral. The signal on my phone was terrible. The office rang at one point to see if I could ask Mohammed to shed some light on the fate of three Israeli soldiers who had apparently been taken prisoner that day in Ramallah. The question puzzled me because while in Nablus I'd been in a bit of a bubble, unaware of news that developed during the day. I could only check the wire in the afternoons.

I rang Mohammed and asked him what he'd heard.

'Oh, they're dead, uncle,' he said over the phone.

'Okay,' I replied and hung up. I rang the office to pass on the news. I didn't expect the reaction I got from the other end.

'They're dead?' one person practically screamed down the line. I hadn't realised the significance. I was going to funerals of Palestinians every single day and it only seemed logical to me that there would be Israeli casualties. I had not been informed of the circumstances under which these men were supposed to have died. Karin rang me soon after and told me to get to Ramallah as soon as I could.

'The deaths of these Israeli reservists could spell the end of the peace process,' she said.

Wow, I thought after hanging up. *Israeli lives really must be more valuable than Palestinians.* There were at least eight Palestinians dying every day since the fighting first broke out, and there had been only a handful of Israeli casualties.

Now suddenly three dead Israeli soldiers could spell the end of the peace process?

Lefteris, after calling the office, had been told to stay in Nablus because there were two other photographers already covering Ramallah. He looked up at me and raised his hands in resignation.

'I'm sorry, I can't come with you,' he said. We went back to the car and I grabbed my small bag, leaving my little red suitcase in the boot, and managed to hitch a ride back to Nablus with a Reuters crew.

In Nablus a sense of impending catastrophe had started to fill the town. There was disquiet among the people, and the word 'Ramallah' was being whispered rather than spoken. Everyone was unsure what fate would befall that town. There was talk of revenge, but no one knew what the Israelis would do. *Would they invade? Would they bomb everything?* It wasn't clear and the uncertainty only heightened everyone's anxiety.

During my time in Nablus I'd been anxious to prove myself, lest people think I was a fraud for not knowing enough about the situation, the players, the history. So I said yes to every request, went everywhere I was asked to go. I was either unaware of the risk or went in spite of it, which happened to be the case this time. Now I faced the logistical dilemma of getting to Ramallah.

Mohammed took me to the taxi stand to see if a cab would take me there. Unsurprisingly, no one was keen to go. We waited an hour and, only after about six people said they needed to get to Ramallah before the end of the day, did one driver decide to take the plunge. I waved nervously to Mohammed from the window; with my flak jacket between my knees, the taxi swung out of the car park and we left Nablus, heading into uncertain terrain.

CHAPTER SIX

Thursday 12 October 2000

after a two-hour journey over small hills and ditches in an old orange Mercedes taxi carrying six Palestinian passengers as well as myself, we arrived in Ramallah. At one point we were stopped by an Israeli roadblock and when they took everyone's ID cards I was worried they wouldn't let me through. I handed over my passport and waited for the reaction. But the soldiers said nothing.

They allowed the taxi to pass after first telling all the male passengers to get out and move some large rocks from the middle of the road. The soldiers could have done it themselves but they didn't; they knew the Palestinians couldn't refuse. The women in the car muttered curses at the soldiers for humiliating the men like this. Fighting with myself to say something and feeling ashamed that I didn't, I kept my mouth shut and my head down. It didn't feel good to stay silent, but this was not the time to speak out.

This was an example of the humiliation the Palestinians said they were regularly subjected to. The Israeli soldiers could do anything they wanted and they were so young.

That's a lot of power in the hands of a kid with a gun. What the soldier chose to do with this power could breed either resentment or trust. It was here, at the checkpoints, that most Israelis came into contact with Palestinians, who would brace themselves for rejection and possible mistreatment. Making a Palestinian move a rock or play a violin or sing a song, just so they could pass through a checkpoint, didn't help anyone.

As soon as we arrived in Ramallah I was lost. I'd come here with Elizabeth to cover that first funeral nearly two weeks earlier, but I was completely unfamiliar with the geography. The centre of Ramallah, the area the Palestinians called al-Manara Square, was buzzing. The shops were open and there were people in the streets. This did not look like a town that had just lynched Israeli reservists.

During my cab ride I had spoken to the office to try to get more information about what had happened. Two Israeli reservists—rather than three, as we'd heard earlier—had taken a wrong turn on their way to an army office in the West Bank and ended up in Ramallah. They had been spotted by Palestinian police and taken to the police station in the centre of town. It was about 100 metres up from al-Manara, the city centre, a roundabout upon which sat four lions facing outwards, watching over the city. Word had spread quickly that there were Israelis in Ramallah, and some rumours also suggested they were undercover operatives. Whether there was truth in these rumours, the stories were sufficient enough to whip men on the streets into a frenzy. They broke into the police station and killed the two men. The exact details of the deaths were never made clear. Whether they were beaten or shot first, no one really knows. What was horribly clear, though, was that the crowd was eager for blood.

To show the seething crowd that the two men were dead,

one Palestinian man flung himself at the window, raising bloodied palms to a crowd that erupted in cheers. In television footage that captured the incident, one of the men's bodies was dumped from a second floor window to the ground and then was beaten, kicked and stomped. The other was dragged out down the stairs and also beaten.

I had been asked to go to the police station to see if I could speak with some of the officers there to find out what had happened. I rang Nasser Nasser, our Ramallah-based photographer, to see where he was. We chose a rendezvous point, a suburb called Beituniya. I was so completely lost I couldn't find a taxi or even the taxi stand. A man walking towards me saw my face and guessed that I was scared.

'You shouldn't be on the street alone,' he cautioned me.

'I have to get to Beituniya.' He nodded.

'No problem.' He stood on the edge of the street and flagged down a taxi. 'Take her to Beituniya,' he said and tapped the door after I got in.

'Thank you,' I said, waving goodbye.

I was wearing my flak jacket now; I was in no mood to take chances. The taxi dropped me off on a hillside in Beituniya, near some apartment buildings. A few minutes later Nasser arrived in his car. I hadn't seen him since the funeral I'd covered with Elizabeth. We wound our way downhill and parked near al-Manara, around the corner from the police station.

'Nasser,' I said. 'We have to go to the police station and talk to the police.' He just looked at me and shook his head.

'There's no one there now, Jamie,' he said. He had witnessed the scene earlier and was pretty shaken. When the two Israeli reservists were killed, many of the photographers and cameramen were harassed by the Palestinian police and the demonstrators. Nasser had had his film confiscated and others had equipment broken. I still had to go to the police station to check it out anyway, despite his reluctance.

I remember getting out of the car and hearing a faint boom. Then a whistle. Then a crash. I steadied myself as the ground moved. *It can't be bombing*, I thought. The last time this happened to me I was in Lebanon, fourteen years old and with my family. We ran into a building as we heard another boom, followed by the whistle, which took about four seconds before there was an enormous crash. I rang the office.

'They're shelling Ramallah,' I stammered.

'Yeah, we're watching it on TV,' one of the staffers said, adding that the rockets had struck the police station. I got off the phone before I could start swearing. I was specifically told to go to the police station to get more information on the lynching—the very building that had just been blown up. I was too angry to feel the irony of being in the middle of a town being shelled while my colleagues were back in the office in Jerusalem, watching it from the safety of their desks. *Why on earth am I doing this? This is bullshit.*

There was a break in the shelling and we could hear people scrambling to the police station to see the damage. Nasser grabbed his cameras and took off. I followed reluctantly and slowly.

An angry crowd swirled in front of the tumbled-down police station, waving fists in the air and chanting furiously. I didn't dare get closer. If they'd been unfriendly before, they'd be positively incensed now, and I was not prepared to risk their ire. I was too much of a target in my flak jacket with 'PRESS' emblazoned on it.

I was on the phone talking to the office, describing the scene, edging as close to the crowd as I could without attracting any attention. Then the mob began to turn, to come down the street in my direction, towards al-Manara. As I spoke on the phone I quickly ducked into a building, where the lobby was filled with people probably just as scared as I was. Then another call came through the line, it was Jocelyn Noveck, my bureau chief.

'Are you okay, Jamie? Where are you? Are you safe?' It was the first time anyone had asked me that. I was so relieved to hear her questions. I told her where I was and she said not to do anything I didn't feel sure about. I looked around at the other people sheltering in the lobby and decided it was safe to stay. I could hear and feel the crowd moving closer and closer. When they reached the building we were in the clamour became deafening; I was shouting down the phone, but Jocelyn said she was having difficulty hearing me. Then the noise ebbed. Tentatively, I stepped out of the building.

I recognised some of my colleagues standing outside. One of them, Ismail, a Reuters soundman, whom I had first met covering the demonstration outside the Arab-Israeli Ministry building in east Jerusalem, told me he had been holding a camera for a colleague and put it down while the lynching took place.

'We couldn't shoot a thing,' he said.

While I was talking to Ismail we suddenly heard the drone of helicopters. Then there was panic in the street and people started running in every direction. My phone battery died, so I took one of Nasser's phones. As I followed him, I got tangled up in what looked like fishing line. I realised it was wire from the rocket. They'd used wire-guided missiles in the attack—the pilot would fire a missile that shot out a wire at the target, and the rocket would be guided by the wire to its mark before exploding. This was one of the reasons why the Israeli shelling had been so accurate. No one had died in that day's rocket attacks. It was an explicit message from the

Israelis to the Palestinians and indeed the rest of the world, that they could strike and kill if they so chose.

I didn't know where I was running to, or what I was running from. There was fear the Israelis would hit the police station again, so people tried to get as far away from that area as possible. But then a crash sounded some distance off and people started shouting.

'They've hit the Muqataa [Yasser Arafat's offices and residence],' several people yelled. So we all started running in that direction to see what had happened.

Then another rocket hit a communications tower. Followed by another crash. I didn't want to be in the street after that. I was completely unsure of where I was going or what the next target was likely to be. I went inside a residential building and hid underneath the stairs while the building on one side and the communications tower on the other side were being shelled.

Thoughts of my family rushed through my head. They would be so anxious. *What am I doing here? I'm from Sydney*, I said to myself. *I'm an Aussie chick who likes to go to the beach, watch rugby union and listen to rock music, and here I am caught in frigging rocket wire in a conflict zone. Could my life be any more different from what it was a month ago?*

My family worried themselves sick about me, utterly terrified about what was going on. I knew they loved me and cared about me, and here I was putting myself in danger—*for what exactly?* This was a question I would come to ask myself repeatedly over the coming days.

After the shelling ended, Nasser and I somehow found each other in the chaos; we headed to the Grand Park Hotel in Beituniya, where I took a room. There I met Peter de Jong, an AP photographer who'd come in from Amsterdam to help out. All departments of production at the AP office had called for extra help—from writers like me, photographers and TV cameramen—to handle the heavy workload. Writers and photographers had arrived from New York, Paris, Cairo and London. More and more people arrived from overseas during the following weeks to be a part of this story, which was growing in profile each day.

Nasser was still recovering from what had been an emotionally exhausting day. We sat in the lobby next to an electrical outlet I'd found so I could recharge my phone. I remember it ringing while we were there; my worried father on the other end of the line.

'You're still in Nablus, right?'

'Yes Dad,' I lied. I was hardly going to tell him the truth.

'Please be careful out there,' he said. God, I could hear the concern in his voice. They were all so worried. And I had no idea what I could possibly say that would ease their minds. Then my phone rang again: It was my ex-boyfriend ringing from Singapore.

'Are you okay? Where are you?' He was the last person I expected to hear from.

'I'm fine, I'm in Ramallah.' I looked over at Nasser, his head in his hands. 'I have to go,' I said quietly into the phone. 'I'm with a photographer who's really freaked out about everything.' His tone changed.

'Oh, you'd better run off to your photographer then.' Those words stung. He'd been insecure about where my career was taking me while we were together, and suspicious of the people I met while travelling. Every time I mentioned the name of a man I had worked with he would accuse me of having slept with them, even though he was the one who'd cheated on me. After the day I'd had, I didn't have the energy to go a round in the ring with him.

'You're kidding me, right?' I said, and hung up.

At dinner that night I ordered a screwdriver, my first alcoholic beverage in weeks, and savoured it slowly. Nablus was very conservative, and Lefteris and I hadn't had a single tipple in the nearly two weeks we were there, out of respect for the town's people and their customs. Besides, we couldn't find any.

&c~9

I remember being awakened early the next morning by the murmur of foreign voices—not Arabic, English or even Hebrew, but French and German. A group of European journalists had taken most of the rooms on my floor and while they philosophised at the top of their lungs, I remembered Peter de Jong's derisive comment as he saw them swaggering down the corridors the previous evening: 'Gucci guerrillas,' he'd sniffed—reporters who arrived to cover conflicts in their best designer labels and meet with friends to solve the world's problems. All I wanted to do was sleep in, but I already had an assignment for that day.

Karin wanted me to find Marwan Barghouti, the local Fatah leader in Ramallah.

'Be his best friend for a couple of hours. Find out his life story, then do a profile on him,' she said to me before I fell asleep the night before.

Barak had been on CNN telling Arafat to order Barghouti to stop the violence, so it appeared the local man's profile was rising in the political stakes. Karin had a mobile phone number for him. I dialled it and actually got through. *Excellent. But who was Marwan Barghouti?*

I had to shout so the person on the other end of the line could hear me. His name was Ahmed and he was Barghouti's bodyguard. He told me Barghouti was talking to the crowd in front of the destroyed police station and that that was where I would find him.

I had to push past people until I finally came to the wall and looked up. I didn't even know which one he was but it should have hit me immediately. A pint-sized man, ferocious in voice and will, was hollering into a megaphone, castigating Israel, admonishing the world's leaders and daring the crowd to be cowed and beaten by the rocket attack. I assumed this was him, and I was right.

'Are you afraid of Barak's tanks and helicopters?' he bellowed.

'No!' the throng of men and boys shouted back to his taunting questions. I waited and took notes as he stood there beside other well-known Ramallah figures, all awaiting their opportunity to rally support.

I don't think he knew what to make of me when we met — an annoying young woman asking him personal questions and following him everywhere. It was highly un-Arab-like behaviour. We hadn't been introduced by someone he knew; he had no idea who I was or where I came from. It didn't matter when I gave him my background, that wasn't the way things were done. But I persisted. As we walked down the street, there was an unending procession of people approaching him to speak to him or just to say hello. He shook hands with everyone like a practised politician. There were back slaps, stomach punches and plenty of kissing.

I found out he was 42 and had four children. When he was seventeen, he went to jail in Israel for six years for belonging to Fatah, which was then illegal. That was where he learnt how to read and speak fluent Hebrew. He became president of the student union at Birzeit University, the breeding ground for Palestinian political action and revolutionary thought. In 1987, he and his family were deported, they spent seven years altogether in Jordan and Tunisia. His wife was a lawyer but it would be more than a year before I met her because, for Marwan Barghouti, history was about to take an unfortunate turn.

He and his entourage bundled into a Jeep to go to the clashes presently being fought outside the City Inn Hotel, near a junction at the bottom of a hill that led out of Ramallah. The Israelis had set up a roadblock there, and it was a daily dance of death at a designated hour for the youths with Molotovs and stones and the soldiers who faced them.

I didn't want to be left behind, so I clambered into the back of the Jeep along with Barghouti's eldest son Qassam, who was fifteen. Chubby, with startlingly blue eyes, he looked over at me indifferently. I smelt a brat. Of course, if your father was the popular unofficial leader of a militia, who travelled everywhere with armed guards and was feted wherever he went, you would feel pretty special too.

We came to the City Inn junction and hovered about 150 metres away from the clashes. Barghouti wanted to get a closer look, but his people kept leading him further away, up a hill. Some news crews spotted him and he obliged them with several sound bites. I patched through to Peter on the two-way and he came up from the clashes to take a couple of snaps of Barghouti, seated on a small brick wall surrounded by people. Barghouti decried the label of militia chief, saying that he really wasn't one. But his demeanour and his statements suggested otherwise.

'I'm the leader, that's right,' he said, then looked at me and smiled. 'Do you think if I told them to leave they would? Who am I that they would listen to me? You think they're here because I tell them to come?'

I suppressed a smile as I looked around. There were

plenty of armed men standing nearby. At one point, a couple of them were snapping ammunition rounds into place, loading them in front of civilian bystanders.

'You know you can't do that here,' Barghouti chided them. 'Do it somewhere else.' *Is he telling them off because there is a reporter present?* I wondered. *Or is he worried about everyone else's safety?*

The demonstrations themselves grew fiercer, until eventually the sound of gunfire rang out. Barghouti's guards pulled him into the entrance of a nearby building but it was too close for their comfort. Shortly afterwards they jumped into their Jeep and sped off. I had enough material for my story so I didn't accompany them, but I noticed the car's plates were the official Palestinian Authority's red-and-white issue. He was an elected lawmaker after all, I recalled. That went some way to justify the extra security presence he had.

As I sat by a closed shop up the road from the clashes I went over my notes. I had become quite accustomed to the sound of gunfire. I wrote in longhand, unperturbed by the trouble unfolding around me. The office called, wanting some 'colour' from the scene. How I came to detest that word! As I described to them over the phone what I saw, gunmen started shooting from across the street. I hung up.

It was inevitable that the shooting would come back in my direction. Before long the Israelis were firing rounds off just up the street from where I was sitting. I scrambled to my feet and ducked behind a parked car. I don't know why I was always convinced that a car would provide enough cover. Perhaps, I reasoned, it was better than nothing at all.

A bunch of schoolboys came and huddled near me as well, or rather stood over me. I thought they were providing me with some form of protection. When the gunfire abated, we all got up and they said to me, 'Come on, *yalla*.' Following them,

I ran up the hill towards safety. While I was still walking with them, my phone rang. The office wanted me to go to a press conference that the Information Minister, Yasser Abed Rabbo, was giving at the ministry. I took down the directions and headed off.

After 30 minutes of walking, stopping and asking directions and walking some more, I realised I wasn't going to find the location any time soon. I saw a car pull over and I hurried over to speak to the man getting out.

'Hi,' I said in Arabic. 'I need to get to the Information Ministry. You know where it is?' The tall man looked at me, then ducked his head back inside the car.

'You going back into the city?' he asked the driver. The answer must have been a positive, because he called over to me and said, 'They'll take you to the ministry.'

'Are you sure?' I asked the guy at the wheel. He nodded. I hesitated for a moment. I didn't really want to get into the car of a complete stranger, in an area which wasn't altogether safe, but the tall guy was looking at me with the car door open. I was also running late for the press conference, so I got in.

The driver asked me, 'What is happening at the ministry? Are you a journalist? Who is giving the press conference?' Relieved to be getting some help I happily answered all the questions. I looked ahead, out the front window as the car wound its way through Ramallah, and then my gaze settled on an object on the dashboard, sitting just on top of the speedometer. Black, metallic, with shiny golden pointy things inside. It dawned on me that it was a magazine for an automatic rifle. The pointy things were bullets. Only then did it occur to me to look at who else was in the car. I slowly turned around and saw two men in the back seat with AK47s standing upright between their knees.

'Hi,' I said, attempting casual conversation. They mur-

mured in response. I turned back around, muttering obsceni-
ties at myself for yet another careless mistake. I never
hitchhiked in Australia, and I don't know what possessed me
to do it here. I trusted a complete stranger with my life in a
town that had only days earlier mercilessly stomped on the
bodies of two army reservists. I had this weird sense of feeling
invulnerable, or something else. I trusted that crazy Arab
hospitality, that you were a guest in their land and they would
treat you accordingly. Foreigners were always welcome. I
don't know why I felt like I could do something like that and
not be in danger. The thought that it might be dangerous only
struck me when I saw my travelling companions.

They took me to the ministry and wished me a pleasant
day, then drove off. I emerged feeling bewildered and point-
edly reminded of my complete naivety. *Is it because I speak
Arabic? Do I have an 'in' through that? They tell me, 'You're one of
us', before inviting me into their homes and giving me tea. Is that why
I trust them so easily?*

Inside the ministry, Abed Rabbo criticised the Israeli
actions and said Palestinians were only defending themselves
and fighting an occupation, comments that would be
endlessly recycled as the violence continued. All the journalists there were wearing professional outfits and immaculate
hair, making me conscious of the clothes I was in as I tried to
brush my hair back with my hands. I'd been wearing the
same clothes since I left Nablus three days ago. I was a mess.
After all that trouble getting to the press conference, I spent
only a few minutes speaking to someone at the office, relaying
Abed Rabbo's quotes, before getting a ride back to the hotel
with a colleague.

The next day I got a call from the office: I could return to Jerusalem. I got a lift to the checkpoint at Ramallah. Ismail, the Reuters soundman, was on the other side ready to give me a ride back to the office. I walked up to the checkpoint, to the soldiers surrounded by people lining up with their ID cards, waiting to be waved through. They saw me approach, I flashed my passport and they nodded at me to pass. Through the dust and the heat I walked over to the other side and slumped into the passenger seat of Ismail's car. He shifted the car into gear and we were on our way.

One chapter of this adventure is over, I thought as we drove back to Jerusalem. I could walk back into that frenzied newsroom and feel satisfied that I had done everything that had been asked of me and I had come out with good stories and details. I did okay and I didn't die. And while I still didn't know so much about this place and the story itself was turning into a nightmare, I could relax just a little. In my own mind I'd just passed my first test.

CHAPTER SEVEN

Friday 20 October 2000

O n my return to Jerusalem I promptly fell ill from exhaustion and was fighting off the flu. While recuperating I got to know most of the new people who'd flown in to Jerusalem to help out. We would all manage to cram around one corner of the bar at Mona's, a restaurant in a building called The Artists House. It was the buzzing place to be. Visiting photographers and war correspondents could socialise there with resident foreign press. They'd trade war stories or talk about a close call they'd had that day, or they'd nostalgically recall days of conflicts past, such as Kosovo and Rwanda.

Much of the foreign press covered the clashes in Ramallah each day—it was only half an hour's drive away—while maintaining their base in Jerusalem. Once when Lefteris and I were covering clashes in Nablus, we watched a television crew drive up towards a checkpoint and set up their equipment. Then the coiffed television reporter stood in front of some demonstrators with his flak jacket on and did his piece to camera. Afterwards they packed up and left. It didn't take more than an hour.

I began to settle into a routine. It became a usual thing that after Friday prayers Palestinians would protest and the protests would turn into clashes. So I covered any demonstrations in Ramallah or east Jerusalem on those days, depending on where they were happening. I'd never get too close, even though I had a flak jacket. I just didn't want to tempt fate. The few times I swallowed tear gas were bad enough for me.

Nothing can prepare you for your first lungful of tear gas. It leaves you choking and struggling to breathe. Your eyes burn and your nose starts running. You can't see. You're not supposed to rub your eyes as that will only make it worse. On one occasion I was standing among demonstrators coughing and spitting after copping some tear gas when a young guy, his head wrapped in a Hamas flag, came up to me and pressed a piece of cotton wool dipped in perfume into my hand.

'Breathe it in,' he said. Eyes streaming, I nodded and thanked him.

'I'd give my eyes so you're not in pain,' he said to me. I spat and dribbled, while marvelling at how so much of the Arabic language is infused with drama.

❦

The meeting in Sharm el Sheik on 17 October 2000, overseen by Clinton and the UN's Kofi Annan, ended but the violence didn't. Both sides declared a ceasefire and agreed to return to negotiations, but the truce didn't hold. Increasingly the clashes involved Palestinian gunmen attacking Israeli soldiers and focused on Jewish settlements and the settlers who lived in them. We were all on suicide-bomb alert after a janitor with explosives strapped to his body rode a bike towards a checkpoint in Gaza, killing himself but not the soldiers. For us that meant no more taking the bus to work. I had always liked to take the bus to work when I lived in Sydney and Singapore. I could gaze out the window and listen to music; it was my 'alone' time and it calmed me. I had just started to enjoy doing that in Jerusalem, but that was now over.

One evening as we sat at The Artists House eating steak at 11 p.m.—my entire lifestyle and schedule revolved around the news now, so eating at odd times was part of my life—we got a call from the office telling us that Beit Jalla was being shelled by rockets. Beit Jalla is a small village just outside Bethlehem in the West Bank. It sits on the side of a hill across the valley from the settlement of Gilo, which Israelis argue is a neighbourhood of Jerusalem. But Gilo was built on land captured in the 1967 war so, in the event of a peace agreement based on pre-1967 borders, it would be returned to the Palestinians. For the people of Beit Jalla, the ever-expanding Gilo was a constant source of frustration, taking up more and more land and moving closer and closer to their village. Har Gilo, or Higher Gilo, was literally on Beit Jalla's doorstep and the nearby Har Homa settlement was encroaching on forest where many Palestinians used to go with their families for picnics.

The night Beit Jalla was shelled was the first time I met Jerome Delay and Laurent Rebours, AP photographers from Paris. Jerome, always smiling, had more energy than anyone I knew. Laurent was almost stereotypically French. He had Elizabeth and I in hysterics as he banged an empty wine bottle down on the bar, expecting the bartender to immediately attend to him with a replacement.

As it was nearly midnight, we didn't know if the office wanted us to go and check out the situation in Beit Jalla immediately or wait till morning. Jerome spoke up quickly, though, as he had friends who lived in Beit Jalla, the Dabdoubs. Jerome's daughter Pauline used to correspond with their daughter Dalia, so he wanted to see how they were. There wasn't anyone other than me from the writers' side there, so I agreed to go with him.

Once inside the car Jerome told me to put on his flak jacket and we sped to Beit Jalla. We telephoned the office to let them know of our movements. Once we passed the Bethlehem checkpoint Jerome drove slowly and left the light on inside the car, so people would know who we were. It was a tad eerie. I don't know how he managed to find the house in the dark but he did. We tripped over rocket wire as we climbed the steps to their door. Jerome pounded on the door and the shocked father, Abdullah, let us in.

I hoped Jerome knew what he was doing. I'd just met him and I wasn't sure we should be here for very long at all. It made me nervous to be in a town streaked with rocket wire and plunged into darkness from power cuts. In hindsight, I realised my first weeks in the Holy Land were filled with missteps and impulsive behaviour. I wasn't being very careful.

The family was sitting in the dark, the children absolutely petrified. It was way past their bedtime but they couldn't sleep. Dalia was wrapped in a blanket and sitting on the floor, her face reflecting the yellow glow of the kerosene lamp that provided the room's only light. Abdullah Dabdoub went to his liquor cabinet and poured each of us a shot of brandy. Jerome took some pictures of the family and after sitting with them for nearly an hour we left to return to Bethlehem.

As we drove slowly towards the checkpoint, we heard yelling. It was raining heavily and I shifted in my seat, agitated. When someone banged on my window, I gave an involuntary shout and nearly hit my head on the car roof.

There were two Israeli soldiers standing next to the car, drenched. I wound down the window to talk to them. They were so young and they were probably as frightened as I was. We spoke briefly and were allowed to move on. I felt sorry for them standing in the driving rain, checking vehicles all night, water dripping from their helmets all over their faces. What a way to spend an evening.

We decided to go to the American Colony Hotel in Jerusalem to have a few calming drinks while Jerome filed his pictures. The American Colony Hotel was an institution. It had a lengthy history—owned by a French family, it was a favourite haunt of famous British actor and raconteur Peter Ustinov; way before my time though. Apart from its world-famous bartender, Ibrahim, who makes the meanest Bloody Marys, it is also where most of the wealthier foreign press hang out. The Colony's prices were in US dollars—a lot of US dollars—and as we, us wire reporters, were mostly paid in Israeli shekels, we would hang out at the much cheaper Artists House for dinner and drinks. We simply could not afford to get drunk at the Colony. At best, we'd be able to have a couple of drinks in the cellar bar or restaurant while checking out the recognisable foreign correspondents who could afford the prices there, such as CNN's Christiane Ammanpour or the BBC's John Simpson.

The Colony was also one of the few hotels in Jerusalem where you could have ham with your breakfast, seven days a week. Diplomats would go there to talk to journalists; though, if you had a secret you didn't want to share with others, it was best to choose someplace else—every wall at the Colony had ears. This was also the scene of some of the earliest Palestinian–Israeli dialogue and many Israelis would go there on Saturdays to eat at the superb restaurant. Like any place that draws journalists and diplomats, it was not uncommon to see a certain degree of debauchery after a long night's drinking. Stories abounded of diplomats dancing with Russian prostitutes at 4 a.m. some nights, everyone ending up naked in the swimming pool other times—and some of these stories were even true.

I got into trouble with my bosses after that trip to Beit Jalla—they didn't like the idea of me traipsing about in the dead of night to a place that was being bombed. I was ordered not to go anywhere without permission from above, which was frustrating. This was when my work and everyday personal life merged. Even my movements during my own spare time were controlled by those 'higher up' because my safety was someone else's responsibility.

One morning I was asked to go to Bethlehem to cover the funeral of a fifteen-year-old boy called Muayed Darwish. I climbed into an APTN Jeep with cameraman Rawhi Rizam and some other crew members who worked with a couple of the Arab satellite channels. We drove through Bethlehem until we reached a camp on its outskirts, high in the hills. Bethlehem was always one of the more beautiful towns for me, with its valleys and hills, lush and green, strikingly contrasted against its forests and clear skies. There was something mesmerising about its natural beauty and the freshness of its air.

At the top of a steep hill we reached the house of mourning. Rawhi and the others rushed off with their equipment; for them, it was imperative to get footage of the body inside the house as the relatives said farewell. It was one of the things on their checklist—body in the house, body in the mosque, procession etc. etc. This was television news at its most basic; it was one of the things I also disliked most about being a journalist as it felt almost sleazy, using other people's grief as a key ingredient in my stories.

I edged up to the house past men seated on white plastic chairs. They sat in rows behind each other under a large canopy, their hands clasped in front of them; many held worry beads and murmured softly to each other. I entered a house full of grieving women—an image that immediately threw me back to another time.

After my grandmother died in 1989 when we were living in Beirut, my elder sister and I were told to go into the main room of my grandparents' house in downtown Christian east Beirut to kiss my grandmother goodbye. I was fourteen years old and my sister Maria fifteen. It was too morbid a gesture for me to even think about, but I agreed to do it, if for no other reason than not to upset my parents and relatives. On that day, Maria and I opened the door into the room where all our aunts, cousins and other female relatives sat in rows, crying, clutching handkerchiefs, their lips quivering. My grandmother was dressed entirely in white, her body lying on something cold—maybe a refrigerator to keep it preserved. I could barely bring myself to look at her. Her eyes were closed and her hands placed together upon her chest. Because I was named after her, the sight of me standing before her sent my aunts into another wave of cacophonic grief. They started calling out my name, again and again, and crying because of that connection. I stumbled as I reached over her body, just stopping myself from touching her to keep my balance. I quickly kissed her hand; as did Maria. Then we got out of there as soon as we could. I will never forget that moment. She was so cold.

I thought of that time as I looked around the room outside Bethlehem. It looked very much the same. Some of the women in the room gestured for me to sit on one of the sofas that were crammed with women. I looked around to see if I could identify a relative of the boy. Little children, their brows furrowed with confusion, were interspersed among the women. Someone pointed out the mother to me and my shoulders slumped as I realised I wouldn't be getting anything from her. It was clear she just wasn't there. I imagined if I'd been in her place, if I were a mother and this had been my fifteen-year-old boy I wouldn't want to deal with the reality of his death either.

As in the case with my grandmother's funeral, I didn't want to be there for a moment longer than I had to. Some of the women started on me when they discovered I was a journalist, attacking the United States and the West for helping Israel.

'You only show the bad things about the Palestinians,' one woman charged. Another woman tried to calm her down, saying I was hardly to blame. After offering my condolences, I quietly excused myself.

By the time I emerged into the sunlight, the male funeral party had already moved on. The chairs were empty, and the canopy cast a shadow over the grey concrete outside the house. I didn't know where to go; there was no sign of any of the male mourners. I began to walk, hoping I would find my way. I'd reached the bottom of the hill when a van filled with young boys drove up next to me. One boy leaned out the window and asked, 'You going to the funeral?' I nodded. He turned to the driver and said, 'Pull over,' then told me to get in.

I couldn't help but laugh at how brazen this boy was. I climbed aboard, clearly not having learned my lesson in Ramallah. I looked around inside the van and saw it was filled with boys, all about fifteen years old. They were Muayed's friends. They were with him when he was killed. Conveniently, the office rang my mobile to ask me to get some comments from boys Muayed's age, telling me how they felt about his dying so young. I told them where I was and the company I was keeping, and they said to stick with them and see what happened.

The boys were planning on going to Rachel's Tomb after the funeral to throw stones. The Tomb, guarded by Israeli soldiers, is about 500 metres inside Bethlehem and had become as much a flashpoint of confrontation between Israeli soldiers and Palestinians as Joseph's Tomb had been in Nablus. Rachel, Jacob's wife, was buried there and many religious Jewish women go to the Tomb to pray for fertility, since Rachel had difficulty becoming pregnant. After years of trying, she finally gave birth to Joseph, the Jewish patriarch they believe to be buried in Nablus. Rachel's Tomb was where Muayed was killed after throwing petrol bombs at the soldiers' guard posts. Early in the conflict the Israeli army declared petrol bombs lethal weapons and said they would draw retaliatory gunfire. The difference between stones and petrol bombs was the choice between rubber bullets and real live bullets in the return fire.

The boys were so young. Issa was tall and skinny. He was driving because it was his father's van. He was fifteen. Abdel Hai seemed to be the leader of the group, even though he was slighter than the rest and only fourteen. He was the brazen one. He turned around in the passenger seat and started firing off questions at me, one after the other.

'Who are you? Where did you come from? Who do you work for? Where do you live?' He barely paused for breath. I shot back.

'What about you? How do you know Muayed?' They all chimed in with answers.

'We played soccer together every morning.'

'He's our friend. We go to the same school.'

'He was the reason we used to all get together every morning to play.'

This little town and the refugee camp they lived in was all they knew. They talked among themselves about how Muayed had made a mistake by getting too close to the soldiers, exposing himself to their fire. His death hadn't really registered with them. One boy, Khader, a cherubic sixteen-year-old, looked over at me with his striking green eyes as he toyed with a slingshot he'd fashioned from a thick elastic band and wood.

'We're going to give them a lesson,' he said as the car hurtled towards the cemetery. The rest agreed.

The office called me again, concerned the boys might be swayed by my presence to put themselves in unnecessary danger. They told me to leave them as soon as I could. I agreed that my staying with them would be irresponsible. I'd become increasingly uneasy during the ride about how their contact with me might influence what they did that day. I had a bad feeling I might be encouraging dangerous behaviour. We'd seen lots of young demonstrators performing for the cameras because they would be able to see themselves in the newspapers and television later on, if they lived that long. Many didn't. Wherever there were photographers and camera crews there were children, especially at the clashes. Most foreign photographers knew little Arabic, but they all knew *sawirni* was 'photograph me' in Arabic, kids yelled it out at them all the time. I'd watch those kids compete for the lenses—who was the most elaborate slingshot thrower? Who got the closest to the soldiers when throwing a rock? They were bare-chested, their T-shirts wrapped around their heads to cover their faces. They were boys playing at a grown-up game with grown-up consequences they didn't understand.

Issa parked the van and everyone jumped out. Once we reached the crowd, the boys seemed to feel their size and shrank within the throng. Their bravado faded in the face of real danger, real guns, real bullets. They stood to the side when bigger, armed men walked by toting automatic rifles. They pointed to handguns tucked into the backs of jeans and wondered to each other what make they were.

'I know someone who's got one of those,' Ahmed said. Abdel Hai slapped him on the back, 'Yeah, so why don't you use it?' I watched them play and punch each other, while keeping an eye on the men moving around them. *It's only a matter of time before they begin carrying weapons*, I couldn't help thinking. *Their childhood has already ended.*

We were standing at the edge of the cemetery, next to a high wall. Muayed would be buried on the other side of this wall. Posters of his face with his close-cropped schoolboy hair were everywhere. That was the biggest reminder for Khader that his friend was no longer around. He wouldn't be wearing his soccer jersey and playing in any games with them any more. He wouldn't be tearing around the neighbourhood in the van with them, talking tough. He wouldn't walk with them to school any more. He wouldn't complain about homework with them.

Men stood over each other and poked elbows into each other's backs as they jostled to secure a good position from which to see Muayed's body being lowered into the family crypt. I spotted Elizabeth taking pictures along with a dozen other photographers. Muayed's father, Osama, wept uncontrollably and was being held back from the edge of the hole. Suddenly Ahmed jumped up and clung to the wall, hoisting himself up. He stood precariously on the edge as Muayed's body was lowered inside the crypt. The clicks of the cameras sounded like a roomful of secretaries typing wildly. Muayed's father fainted and was taken away by a group of men. When Ahmed jumped back down, tears filled his eyes.

'Are you okay?' I asked. He nodded, blinking back tears. Right then, he decided not to go with his friends to Rachel's Tomb. 'I'm the youngest in my family. I don't want to see my father behave like that,' he said.

Abdel Hai scoffed.

'Ahmed's afraid,' he said and they all began walking towards Rachel's Tomb with most of the crowd. The photographers were heading in that direction too, to take shots of the inevitable clashes.

I was torn. I didn't want any of the boys to go at all. Seeing Muayed's father break down like he did, I couldn't imagine how I'd feel, even after spending just this small amount of time with these boys, if something happened to them as well. Issa then decided not to go to the Tomb either.

'I have to take the car back to my father,' he said, and agreed to give Ahmed a lift back to their neighbourhood. I looked at Abdel Hai and Khader and told them I wasn't going to the Tomb, so if they were doing it because they thought I would write about it, they could forget it — I was leaving.

'I don't want to come tomorrow and write a story about your funeral,' I added before I turned to walk away, hoping Abdel Hai would get the message. Finally, he relented.

'I'm only going to watch,' he said.

'I don't care,' I said, shrugging my shoulders. 'You do what you want, I'm leaving.'

'Okay, okay,' he said. He walked back some way with me before I met up with Elizabeth and got a ride back to Jerusalem with her.

I don't know if he did go back to the Tomb and the scene of the clashes that followed. Maybe the pull to be involved was too great. Khader, beneath his boyish exterior, seemed determined to exact some sort of revenge, however futile, for his dead friend. I was upset for quite a while after that day and I kept an eye out for the names of people killed in clashes in Bethlehem. I never saw Abdel Hai's name, nor that of his friend Khader. Several months later I saw Issa again. He remembered me and I asked how he and his friends were. He said they were all fine.

I wonder who was the stronger in the end, whether Ahmed was shamed and coerced into participating or whether Abdel Hai backed down. Maybe, as boys do, they got bored and looked for another diversion. Maybe they just went back to playing soccer.

CHAPTER EIGHT

November 2000

O ne afternoon, I was sitting in the newsroom in Jerusalem when we heard that a car bomb had exploded at the Mahane Yehuda market off Jaffa Road, just blocks from our office. The market, called the *shouk*, offered a glittering array of fruit and vegetables, fish, meat and clothes. Both Arabs and Jews worked there. I would walk past the market on my way home at night, tripping over shopping bags and hawkers selling strawberries and eggs on the rim of Jaffa Road. People would cram onto the narrow footpath, waiting for buses or getting last-minute groceries before heading home.

The shops that looked out onto Jaffa Road were bakeries and the aroma of the fresh bread and cakes tugged at my sensibilities, without fail. Everything looked so delicious—the pastries curled into buns sitting in rows, the loaves of bread that smelled of cinnamon or zaatar, the herb I loved in Lebanon and found was widely consumed by both Israelis and Palestinians, and so much more: doughnuts, creamy chocolate cakes, bagels, croissants. I nearly swooned over the smells.

The car loaded with explosives had been parked in a side alley. Two people had been killed, including the daughter of a prominent hardline Israeli politician. It was the first lethal car bomb of this still-young intifada. After that we were cautioned to be vigilant when in crowded places. It was unnerving. I didn't go to cover the story, which was just as well. I don't know how I would have coped with walking past the market after that. I doubt I would have been able to look at all the food without imagining dead people there too.

⌒∽∾⌒

As part of the AP's efforts to protect its staffers, I was scheduled to fly to London for a hostile environment training course by former British marines on a country estate somewhere in the middle of England. The day before I was due to fly out, I was in the office and discovered that I'd lost my wallet. In a panic, I called every credit card company and bank to cancel all my cards. In the middle of this personal distress, I was recruited to go to Beit Sahour, where Israeli helicopters had just taken out three people in a rocket attack—only one of them, Hussein Abayat, was the target, but two women had also been killed.

It was a blisteringly hot day. I had to navigate past a checkpoint in Gilo and then walk a kilometre carrying the heavy flak jacket before I finally reached Nasser Shiyoukhi, who was waiting for me at the other side.

'Do you want to see where it happened?' he asked me. I nodded, and we sped off.

At the top of a steep hill groups of people walked up and down, murmuring to each other. I could hear them recounting the incident, pointing to a dark crater in the ground.

There was still a whiff of burnt tyres in the air. We parked outside the house Abayat had been visiting before he was killed. Abayat was a local Fatah leader, one of Arafat's men. The Israelis said he was behind the killings of three Israeli soldiers. A group of journalists were standing outside the two-storey building, doing their best to speak to a man who was describing the scene.

I noticed a woman standing close by and approached her. She said her name was Jahane Shaabat. She could have been Abayat's girlfriend, she wouldn't say, but Hussein Abayat had come to visit her. His friends had loitered by his green pick-up truck while he sat out on the terrace with her, drinking strong Arabic coffee while her aunt was present. During their conversation they had looked up at the Israeli helicopters in the sky and wondered what they were doing hovering overhead.

'We were only joking about them, then I took my aunt away as he had to leave,' she said, her dark hair pulled into a ponytail, arms folded tightly over her chest. Abayat then climbed into his truck along with his friends and as they pulled out of the driveway a rocket slammed into the vehicle, killing Abayat. The man speaking with the other correspondents was showing them around the scene. He pointed out the spot where the missile had hit. One of the men in the car with Abayat had escaped with minor injuries. The other was under police guard in a Palestinian hospital with severe injuries.

Another missile had been fired but it missed Abayat. It had landed in the middle of the street, and two women in their 50s were killed. The talkative man pointed to a wall near the driveway of Jahane Shaabat's home. I could see singed grey hair stuck to the wall and blood, presumably that of the women, sprayed onto the brick. It made me want to vomit.

They were just two innocent women. I could imagine them in their shawls and black dresses standing and gossiping when they were struck down.

These were new tactics by the Israelis and the Palestinians. The Palestinians had used a car bomb and now the Israelis had used what they called their 'targeted killing' policy. Instead of trying to calm things down, both sides were ratcheting things up. No signs of a truce. No signs that anyone was willing to compromise.

The Israeli government, famed for its 'long arm' that hunted down attackers no matter how much time has passed, was keen to spill details on how it found Abayat. Officials made no apologies for the deaths of the two women or the other wounded civilian. The attack provoked heavy criticism from Washington, particularly as Clinton was still trying to bring the conflict to a close through mediation.

Later, at the hospital, we tried to get more information. There were plenty of people standing around but none of them seemed willing to speak to us. I had to push aside my own discomfort and concentrate on the job—getting upset about someone's brutal death would only slow me down. I still had a story to get.

While we spoke to one man we had approached, I spotted a plastic bag and some bloodied clothes left lying in the corner. I had no idea who they belonged to and no one else would tell me. Another witness said he had seen chunks of flesh flying everywhere after the rockets struck. *Are there bits of flesh in that bag?* I tried to ignore the thought and concentrate on the man's words. Once I got enough details, I left.

When we congregated for the hostile environment course in Hertfordshire, England, on 8 November I couldn't escape the irony that I was in a simulated hostile environment after being plucked from a real one only a day earlier. Many of the people there had also just been in Jerusalem with me — Peter de Jong, Laurent Rebours and Eyal Warshevsky, the Jerusalem photographer. (Incidentally, my wallet had been in Eyal's car, something I discovered at the end of my day in Beit Sahour.) On our first day on the course we learned some bad news: one of our photographers, a woman named Yola, had been shot in the stomach while covering a relatively benign feature story in Bethlehem. She'd somehow got caught up with some demonstrators and come under Israeli gunfire. Eyal took the news badly, particularly given that Yola had been filling in for him.

'I gave her my car, my flak jacket and I said, "You're me this week",' he told me. Suddenly the idea of a course on how to stay safe in war zones never seemed more timely. Yola suffered extensive internal injuries and after a long and tortured recovery eventually returned to photographing war zones again.

One of the most eye-opening experiences for all of us during the course was the ballistics demonstration. The instructors, many of them former officers with the Royal Marines, were excellent shots. They'd set targets from several hundred metres away: a helmet, a car door, a house door, a steel beam, a concrete wall, a flak jacket, a tub of water meant to symbolise a person, because we are three-quarters water. And they fired different weapons — handguns, submachine guns, sniper rifles — at each of them. We learnt several useful things from this exercise.

You have exactly ten seconds to get the hell away from a concrete wall if you are taking shelter behind it, as it practically dissolves under ten seconds of automatic gunfire. A flak jacket will save you from one bullet only and if it doesn't have a protective cushion, the kinetic energy of the bullet could prove dangerous as well. If your attacker was a good shot, you had practically no chance of surviving behind any of the surfaces, particularly a car door, as is so often used by movie cops—and myself as I noted with resignation. Secure your exit; always know how you're going to get out of a situation when you're going in. No quote is worth your life.

I did have one truly terrifying experience during the course. We'd been warned that we would be 'kidnapped' at one stage, and I'd heard stories from other people who'd put chairs against their bedroom doors at night to stave off would-be assailants. I think the course convenors wanted to do it while we were still relatively clueless. So on the very first day they split us into two groups and said we were going to do a first-aid exercise. Suddenly balaclava-clad men pulled everyone out of our car and I had my face shoved into the dirt, where I lay for what seemed an eternity but was probably only about five minutes. It was probably not the best time for me to undergo this exercise—my memories of Beit Sahour were still fresh in my mind and I found the whole scenario very alarming. I remember saying to myself when a straw bag was pulled over my head, *This is England. This is a game. You're safe.* But I was terrified and it brought home to me how completely unprepared I would be in a situation like that.

'That is the only time we will lie to you this week,' said Mick, one of the instructors after the kidnap exercise. And he was right. It was a good week, and being the only woman among fifteen men, I was a bit spoiled.

A group of us made off one afternoon with a bunch of apples from the cafeteria to feed some horses we'd spotted in a field. The grounds of the estate were beautiful; we spotted pheasants and hares in the bushes. I also had the luxury of a weekend in London, where I caught up with friends, saw a Dali exhibition and—dare I say it, as an Israel-based journalist—ate lots and lots of pork.

～∽✥∾～

By this time I'd moved into a small apartment in an area called Baka, near the German Colony but I didn't really spend a lot of time there. Elizabeth lived in the apartment downstairs and we'd hang out together if we were both home at the same time. I'd sit with her in the cocoon-like living room of her apartment, looking at the dark and ghoulish paintings on her walls and listening to loud Latino music. Or we'd watch DVDs and munch on popcorn she'd flavoured with hot sauce and lemon juice, something she swore was typical of Guadalajara in Mexico, her hometown. She could always tell when I was awake because she could hear me padding about above her. She used to bound up the stairs, burst through the front door and make straight for the fridge. She'd fling open the door and sigh, 'Man, you have NO food!' It was the same thing every time.

I never seemed to have any food in stock. The only thing permanently available was the bottle of vodka I had in the freezer and I occasionally had a tub of ice cream. Whenever I did buy any food, it was always eaten in the one sitting. We would gorge on hummus out of its packet, smeared with chilli paste and downed without looking back. Despite the shouk's temptations, the only sweet thing I had a weakness for was Haagen Daaz French Vanilla ice cream and that never lasted long in my fridge.

It was really best that I not explain my crazy diet to my parents when they rang. My father sounded like a commercial then showing on Australian television, in which a father rings his daughter who's moved out of home to see if she is eating right.

'I just want to know that my little girl is looking after herself,' the father would say. And the daughter would respond, 'Yes Dad, your little girl is looking after herself.'

My father and I would laugh on the phone every time we went through this routine. I missed my family a lot and I didn't want to tell them what was going on or how I was dealing with things. Not very well, I had to admit, but I couldn't tell them that; they were already worried enough. And I wish I hadn't had to tell them that I wouldn't be coming home for Christmas either, because that really hurt them.

I wanted someone to visit me. I was totally alone and it was ruining me. My friends who'd promised to visit were freaked out by the violence and put off their trips. No one knew if it would end or if it would get worse. I grew resentful. Elizabeth's mother had come and stayed with her for a couple of weeks and I felt that the people who said they cared about me should make the same sort of effort, but no one did. Phone calls and emails were sporadic, and most of the time I didn't even know what to say to everyone. I felt they wouldn't understand; I barely did. I couldn't blame them because at the same time, even if they could come and visit, I may not have been able to spend any decent amount of time with them since things were so busy at work.

I spent a lot of time alone and quite often there were days when I would return to my apartment, kick off my shoes and slump onto the couch and just cry. The pile of shoes began to accumulate at the door, making entry tricky. It was everything at once—homesickness, confusion, sadness,

fear, anxiety. Before leaving Singapore I'd ended a relationship that was borderline abusive in its final days, but now
I had no one to lean on. There was nothing familiar in my
new life and I couldn't talk to my new colleagues about
my feelings of loneliness and despair. Many of them were
veterans and had either developed mechanisms to deal with
it or were putting on a show of bravado. *Is this the life of a
foreign correspondent? Because this isn't how I want to live.*

Among my neighbours was a family of French Israelis and
I befriended their son, Raymond, who was a couple of years
younger than me. I'm a bit of an insomniac so we would often
go for midnight strolls in our quiet Jerusalem neighbourhood. Through the darkness we'd walk past many of the old
Arab residences that belonged to families who were forced to
leave in 1948. It was a mixture of nostalgia and eeriness,
strolling under arches of jasmine and taking in the moonlit
stone facades of these enormous structures that rose long
before I arrived on this planet.

Raymond's mother was a cook at the official residence
of President Moshe Katsav and I would sometimes spot her
in the background of television shots. She'd be handing out
drinks at government functions. As far as she was concerned,
I was a bad fellow-tenant. Everyone was supposed to clean
the stairs in the building once a month but because I was
often away I neglected to do my share. She never let me
forget it. She could speak no English and I could speak no
Hebrew and I never stopped regretting telling her I could
speak French. She would catch me on occasions as I was
about to head off early and wearily to an assignment, flak
jacket in one hand, helmet in the other, and tell me off.

'*Vous jamais les nettoyez!*' she'd cry: 'You never clean them!'

When I did actually manage to mop the stairs, she would
come out on the landing and stamp her foot, complaining that

I hadn't done a good enough job. It was, of course, the least of my concerns.

～∞～

Jerome and I went to Hebron towards the end of November for Sarah's Day. This is the occasion when the pages of the Torah relating to Sarah, Abraham's wife, are read and everyone goes to her tomb to pray. The Tomb of the Patriarchs, where Sarah, along with Abraham, Isaac and Jacob are said to be buried, was in the centre of Hebron. I'd never been to Hebron before and I was keen to see what it was like.

Hebron is one of the more incendiary places in the Israeli–Palestinian conflict. The Jews who live there have a reputation for being the most extreme settlers, vowing never to leave the Palestinian city. Even though they are surrounded and outnumbered, they rule the area and terrorise the Palestinian residents. Some 400 of the hard-core religious settlers lived in two- and three-storey buildings in the centre of the city, surrounded by soldiers, who are surrounded by 30 000 Palestinians. It was Area C (Palestinian area controlled by Palestinians) inside Area A (Palestinian area controlled by Israelis), and there had been discord and a history of killings between the two populations for decades. It was a place where the settlers really had the upper hand, as I was about to discover for myself, in a most unusual way.

We drove into the centre of Hebron, where the massive fort-like building housing the Tomb sits on a small hill. This building also contains a large mosque, which had been closed to Muslim worshippers since the beginning of the present intifada. There was a small path that led up the hill to the entrance. Nearby were parked border police Jeeps. I also noticed a police station and a kosher take-away cafeteria.

Yellow Israeli licence plates were on all the cars parked in the narrow roads and steep alleys around the building. Pilgrims covered the hill and filled the car park. Fathers and mothers clutching their children's hands clambered up towards the structure. I looked around me and saw that the streets were empty. For the Palestinian population, there was a curfew — no one was allowed to leave their homes while the commemorations were on, to ensure the Israelis' security. It didn't seem fair to me. I followed the pilgrims as I wanted to know what the worshippers thought about the curfew.

Jerome went off to take some pictures and I decided to get a better look. I stepped onto the gravel path and walked past a border policeman, who then ran to catch up with me and spoke to me in Hebrew. 'I don't understand you,' I told him.

'You can't be here,' he said back in English.

'Why not?' I asked.

'Because, that's the rule,' he said blankly.

'What rule?' I asked.

'You can't stand here. This is the rule.' I looked down at my feet.

'Here? Why can't I stand here?' *This is ridiculous.* He pointed to the grass.

'You can stand there,' he said. If he didn't look so serious I would have sworn he was joking. I was getting annoyed.

'I can't stand on the footpath, but I can stand on the grass?' I asked. Because I'd raised my voice, a couple of Hassidic Jews came over.

'You can't be standing here today,' one man said in an American accent. 'Only Jews are allowed to stand here today. This is our holy day, only Jews can be here.' I don't think I could have raised my eyebrows any higher, not unless I'd had toothpicks to prop them up. I couldn't believe it.

About five men were standing around me now so I tried a different tack. I asked the American his name.

'Shimon,' he replied but he wouldn't give me his surname. He said he was from Chicago.

'What do you think about the fact that Jewish visitors are able to roam around freely while the Palestinians of Hebron are housebound?' I asked him. His answer was quick, sharp and unapologetic.

'The people of Hebron brought this situation upon themselves. They shouldn't be throwing stones and firebombs at us,' he replied.

'And you think it's fair for Palestinian families to be stuck in their homes while Jewish children ride scooters through the empty streets, skipping and playing with their friends?' I was being openly confrontational.

'This is our land. We conquered it. It belongs to us. God gave it to us,' he said. The others murmured and nodded their heads in assent. I wrote down the quotes and walked away, trying to shake off the disgust creeping over me.

It was such a foreign feeling for me to have to contend with. I lived in Australia, a melting pot of different cultures and ethnicities. While racism existed it was never as explicit as this, or maybe I just hadn't been exposed to it. My high school had born-again Christians, Muslims, Protestants and atheists, but we were all Australians and were treated as such. To deny people their basic right to open their windows and step outside their doors because of their nationality was extremely racist to me, regardless of the security situation. What I found most distasteful was that people were basing their actions on religion, and the fundamental principles of all religions were steeped in morality and peace and respect for humankind. It didn't wash with me, using a supposedly moral standpoint to drum home a political point, no matter the cost.

One of my friends back in Sydney, who'd visited Jerusalem many years before I'd arrived, sent me an email one day, in which he mused about religion's pull in one of the world's holiest places.

'Don't you find that being in such a place can put you off religion entirely?' he wrote. It was true. I often had to stop and remind myself that this conflict used holy places as weapons, as battle scenes, as blackmail. The more each side spoke of how moral it was compared to the other side, the more I began to lose faith in everyone's sense of morality.

I met up with Jerome and we walked through the empty streets of the centre of Hebron to the other side of the Israeli cordon. As I walked through the curfewed area I could hear noises coming from inside the houses—someone had a television on, there was a baby crying, pots and pans were being banged about in a kitchen. It was like walking among ghosts. The windows were closed and the curtains were drawn. I made my way slowly on. Once we crossed the cordon, however, we were transported to another world. A market was in full swing.

'Tomatoes, tomatoes!' one man shouted. Men stood in doorways and greeted us. I nodded and moved on. Jerome, inevitably, was accosted by children who asked to be photographed.

'Take our picture, take our picture,' they said. Having lived and worked here for years before moving back to his native Paris, Jerome knew exactly what they were saying and would even repeat it back to the children.

'Look,' he said to me, pointing up. There was a canopy of wire fencing over the market stalls, and behind the houses I could see whitewashed buildings. 'It's a settlement,' he said.

'It's not!' I stopped and stared, unbelieving. A three-storey building with sandbagged windows stood right in the middle of this bustling populace. 'That's it?' I asked, pointing.

I wondered at how these two peoples could live side by side while in such conflict. If it weren't for the sandbags, a settler could stand at the window and watch the activity below. Their wet laundry could drip onto the canvas covering the stalls. But they weren't just living side by side, they were living on top of each other. I then realised there was no proper system to the curfews or the cordons, except that they operated around the settlements and could be imposed at any time. Since the settlements were smack bang in the middle of the Palestinian population the slightest disruption caused major upheaval. One street could be closed while the next was open. One neighbourhood could be under curfew while around the corner people could come and go freely.

Jerome bought some Arabic music cassettes at the market and we met up with Nasser Shiyoukhi briefly. We came out to another section of the cordon, where there was a gate, and further up, an Israeli checkpoint. I walked up to the soldiers on my own and one of them stood to meet me.

'Where are you from?' I asked.

'Haifa.' He tipped the brim of his helmet and flashed me a wide smile. He was cute. I smiled back. I guess he didn't see many friendly girls out there. He was about 20, a para-trooper. His mates looked up from where they were sitting inside their tent to check me out.

'This must be such a drag for you,' I said. 'Shouldn't you be on a beach somewhere?'

'That would be nice,' he said.

'Do you want to be here?' I couldn't help asking.

'Well, no. Not really, but we don't really have a choice,' he replied. It was compulsory for everyone over eighteen to serve in the army. Some people were able to escape the duty—many Hassidic Jews did not serve, a fact that riled secular Israelis.

When I said goodbye to the soldiers I walked back through the gate to the market area to rejoin Jerome. I peeked into a paint shop and saw a man sitting at the counter, gesturing for me to come in.

'*Ahlan wa sahlan,*' Amar Abu Manshour said to me. 'You're most welcome.' It was a typical greeting from Arabs. He said his cousins lived on the other side of the gate and he rarely saw them.

'How can they live like that?' I asked.

'Life has always been difficult for Palestinians living in this area,' Amar said. 'They're used to it.'

CHAPTER NINE

Thursday 30 November 2000 to mid-January 2001

t was Elizabeth's 30th birthday at the end of November and we celebrated with dinner at The Artists House. It was the first time I'd actually bothered with my appearance. We both wore make-up and skirts, forgoing our usual combat pants or jeans and bare faces. Some of the guys didn't even recognise us. A few who hadn't paid any attention to me before suddenly wanted to take me out for a drink. I stayed aloof and dismissive. I'd sworn off men after my last relationship because I didn't believe they were sincere or could be trusted. And here they were proving me right.

Jerome and I had slipped out during dinner to rush to the Supersol, the 24-hour supermarket on Agron Street, opposite the American Consulate in west Jerusalem. We bought a couple of soft porn magazines for Elizabeth, plus some sparklers, before heading back. By this stage we knew Dudu, one of the restaurant's owners, rather well. He turned down the lights while we lit the sparklers and we all sang 'Happy Birthday'.

It was a good night. Afterwards, we went to Tzouf, a nightclub near the cinematheque, a trendy movie theatre, to dance. I had a crush on one of the bartenders there, Itamar, a lanky Israeli who would DJ and charm every girl in the room. Elizabeth and Jerome would tease me, but I'd laugh it off. I didn't mind; I didn't want anything serious.

We had so many good times at that club, often not leaving before two or three in the morning when they were closing up shop. Itamar and Avi, another bartender who ran the place with him, would sometimes pour us shots of vodka spiced with hot peppers or an Armagnac and we would continue to talk with them as the rest of the staff turned the lights up and began stacking chairs. Once we took the British Royal Marines from the hostile environment course out with us; they were then in Jerusalem to give a shorter version of the course to local staff who'd been unable to get to Hertfordshire. It was murder trying to match them drink for drink. When we went clubbing, they were the odd men out. Standing stiffly against the walls with their beers gripped firmly against their chests, they refused to dance and laughed at every attempt to drag them onto the dance floor.

I went to Ramallah on 23 December 2000 to see Marwan Barghouti again. He gave a press conference at which he called for change in the way the intifada was run. Was this an implicit criticism of the Palestinian Authority, his meal ticket? He sat smiling throughout most of the briefing; the room was full of reporters and he was happy to answer questions. It seemed a subtle bid for power.

While continuing to kowtow to Arafat and his untouchable authority, Barghouti was advocating for the PA to include other groups — Hamas, Islamic Jihad, the Popular Front for the Liberation of Palestine — in discussions about the intifada and its future. These were groups that did not recognise the foundation on which the PA and Arafat's leadership were based.

Hamas had dismissed out of hand the Oslo Accords that recognised Israel as a state and its borders as those gained after the 1967 war. It had always pushed for more than the restitution of the pre-1967 borders in any kind of resolution to the conflict, in fact they demanded the eradication of Israel as a state and the return of all the refugees, their descendants and their relatives. Their position had always been more radical, as had their methods. Fatah and Tanzim were restricting their militancy to outside the Green Line — the name given to the 1949 armistice line that defined the borders of pre-1967 Israel — inside the West Bank and Gaza, the disputed areas the Palestinians wanted Israel to leave. The United Nations had also issued resolutions for Israel to withdraw back to the pre-1967 borders, and has never recognised the land grab. It refers to the Palestinian areas as the Occupied Palestinian territories. Hamas and Islamic Jihad made no such distinction and had advocated attacks on Israel proper. Their reasoning was that Israelis should not know any kind of peace or security while the Palestinians were living under occupation. So, while the Tanzim were for drive-by shootings of settlers and checkpoint ambushes, Hamas and Islamic Jihad wanted to send suicide bombers into the heart of Israel, beyond the Green Line.

It was a momentous time in world politics. Clinton's tenure in the White House had come to an end and the close-fought presidential election in November 2000 had resulted in a recount in Florida with George W. Bush emerging as the eventual winner. Many Israelis and Palestinians were downcast at this result. Bush seemed to be a man who would not be engaged in their conflict as earnestly or as wholeheartedly as Clinton had been. For the Israelis it was a double blow: with Joseph Lieberman's candidacy on the Democrats ticket it had seemed possible that an Orthodox Jew might be admitted for the first time into the White House as the Vice-President of the United States.

There was going to be one last-ditch attempt at negotiations. The Palestinians and the Israelis were planning to go to Taba which was located on the border of Israel and Egypt and had been recently handed back to Egypt. I was asked to go with Dina Kraft, a Hebrew-speaking staffer, and Michel Euler, a Swiss photographer who'd come in from Geneva to help out. Travelling into Egypt was surreal.

After our short flight from Tel Aviv to Eilat, at the southern tip of Israel, we took a taxi from the airport to the border, a 25-minute drive. The area reminded me of the Gold Coast in Queensland—hotels galore, overdeveloped and maintained strictly with the tourist dollar in mind. Pulling our suitcases behind us, we made our way through Israel's passport control and over into Egypt's. The erratic bureaucracy that hounds most Arab government procedures was wonderfully apparent among the customs officers at Taba's passport control. In true Arab fashion, there was a queue for everything. We stood in line to get tickets to take our bags through X-ray. Then we joined more queues to have our passports taken, to fill out our declarations, to hand them in and finally to retrieve our passports. On top of this, paranoia ensued once Michel's satellite phone made its way through the X-ray machine. They'd clearly seen his equipment—computer, cameras, tripod, ladder etc.—but once his sat-phone set their machine bleeping, they made him take everything apart, adding nearly an hour to our waiting time.

The Taba Hilton was only ten minutes' walk from the passport control. Once we got there, however, we learnt that the talks had been called off. We couldn't make it back onto a flight that same day even if we wanted to, so we decided to stay there for the night. The next morning we scheduled an afternoon flight and went down to the beach to sunbake.

I was determined to swim, even though everyone told me I was mad even to try. It was November, my friends and colleagues said, the water will be freezing. I laughed them off and waded in anyway—after all, the Pacific Ocean of my home city isn't exactly tepid. As I got further and further into the water I began to smile wider and wider; it was beautiful. The water of the Red Sea was just perfect, the kind of cold that invigorates you. It was sapphire in colour, surrounded by the red-brown jagged mountains of the Sinai. I floated on my back for as long as I could, soaking up the moment. I felt glad to be alive and lucky to be in what is surely one of the most beautiful places on earth.

❧

Christmas arrived and I was feeling really homesick. I couldn't have conversations with my parents and sisters without crying. I hated being away from them, especially at this time of year. I'd listen, smiling and crying at the same time, as they talked about the different presents they were getting each other, My sister Stefanie, who was nine years younger than me, especially made me sad. I was always away at important times of the year as far as she was concerned, and she missed me. In Sydney the whole family would always go to midnight mass on Christmas Eve and then rush home afterwards to open our presents, wading through the wrapping paper to thank each other for our gifts. It was our own family tradition, and I would miss it again this year, as I had the year before when I was covering the new millennium in Singapore.

I told myself that I would at least go to midnight mass in Bethlehem, if for no other reason than to be able to tell people that I had been there for the 2000th anniversary of Jesus' birth. It was raining heavily that night. Rainwater flowed through the streets as I tried to hail a taxi. Soldiers at the entrances to Bethlehem restricted movement in and out of the town to Palestinians with the right travel permits and foreigners. I needed to get a taxi to take me as far as the checkpoint but that proved to be quite a task. I was now getting used to being rejected by taxi drivers once I'd told them of my destination and then scoffing at the preposterous prices they were charging. Tonight, though, I didn't really have a choice. So I agreed to let a taxi take me to the checkpoint for the princely sum of 50 shekels, about US$12, double the regular fare. I must have had the word 'sucker' imprinted on my forehead, I thought as I slumped, soaking wet, into the back seat.

On the other side of the checkpoint I stood shivering in the rain, waiting for Ibrahim Hazboun to pick me up. He was covering the mass for work because Arafat was to attend. Palestinians were barred from travelling outside their own towns, but there was a tacit agreement between the Israelis and the Palestinians to allow Arafat to travel wherever he wanted, including overseas.

When we got to the Church of the Nativity we had to go through metal detectors and leave our mobile phones outside.

I looked at the surging crowds of people handing over their phones and the Palestinian police officers juggling different contraptions and handing out tickets to recover them later. I hesitated and looked at Ibrahim.

'They are *so* going to lose them,' I whispered. He smiled and showed me the extra phone he'd stashed in his pocket — he needed it to file his report to the office. He took mine with his and thrust them together into the policeman's hand, taking a ticket in return.

'Leave it to God, Jamie,' he said as he ushered me inside.

There was nowhere to sit. Nuns, priests, tourists and locals were jammed into the pews. Many leant against the walls while others sat on the marble stone floor, waiting for the service to begin. A German family stood together; I could hear them whispering to each other. One of the little girls was already fast asleep and her father patted her as she lay on his shoulder. He looked over at me and smiled.

There were photographers everywhere of course, waiting for Arafat to arrive. When he did, he got a rousing welcome. I strained to get a glimpse of him; it was the first time I'd ever seen him in the flesh and I was curious to see how big he was and how much he really shook. He seemed a constant quivering mess on television — observers had long speculated that he had Parkinson's disease but his doctors had always sent him off with a clean bill of health. He did look after himself; he was 75 and he exercised every day. He was smaller than I expected. He seemed to be hidden somewhere under that keffiyeh; it covered so much of him.

As I watched the service, different parts of which took place in French, Arabic, Latin and English, I thought I saw someone familiar standing behind Arafat. I stood on my tiptoes to get a better look. I wasn't sure so I tugged at Ibrahim's sleeve.

'Is that Mohammed Dahlan?' I asked, naming one of the Palestinian Authority's principal negotiators and pointing. Ibrahim looked over the rows of people.

'I'll go check,' he said and walked off. Soon after he came back, a smirk tugging at his face.

'Yes, it's Dahlan. He must have just come back from Washington. Arafat is going to make him sit through the mass before he can leave.'

I swallowed a giggle. Dahlan, a devout Muslim, had to sit through one of the holiest rituals in the Christian calendar because Arafat wanted a full debriefing of his trip to Washington. He must have come straight from the airport. Only a day earlier President Clinton—a lame duck president but in charge nevertheless because of the voting recount in Florida—had outlined his vision for peace in the Middle East. This was referred to thereafter as the Clinton Proposal, just as the Mitchell Commission had been created out of the Sharm el Sheik meeting in October. This was a time when there was a mushrooming of peace documents, reports and proposals. It became a major task for us journalists just to keep track of them all.

It was painful for me on this Christmas Eve to look around and see families sitting together. I was falling apart. I cried during the service, keeping my head bowed so no one could see. But Ibrahim noticed and squeezed my arm.

'You miss your family, don't you?' he asked. I could only nod.

After mass, we bumped into some of Ibrahim's sisters. They were tall like him, and absolutely stunning. I joked that he couldn't be related to them because they were all so beautiful.

'What happened to you, then?' I asked, as they laughed.

I was feeling so maudlin, I needed to lift my mood. I knew

that very soon he would be going home to his family, while I would be returning to an empty apartment. There would be no drowning in wrapping paper for me this year. He dropped me off at home, then waved goodbye and rushed back to be with his family.

The next day didn't feel like Christmas on the streets of Jerusalem. As I walked to work along Jaffa Road, I noticed it was just another day. Elizabeth had gone home for Christmas and most of the visiting foreign press had returned to their homes in their own countries to spend the holiday with their families. Perhaps it was better that Christmas wasn't such a big deal here—the thought made it easier for me to get through it on my own.

On that Christmas Day I had to return to Bethlehem to meet Lefteris. We were to cover a group of pilgrims re-enacting the journey of the three wise men, who had followed a star across fields and valleys to come to a manger in Bethlehem to pay homage to a newborn king. But this year Manger Square was deserted and there were no lights. I'd gone in the week leading up to Christmas to report that Bethlehem's Palestinian mayor had cancelled the festivities that would have made 2000 a bonanza year for the city. Only months before the violence began, they had been expecting pilgrims by the busload, as had happened when Pope John Paul II visited the holy city in March 2000. Now the souvenir shops were stacked with mother-of-pearl icons and rosary beads and crucifixes, but there were no customers, so many had shut their doors.

Israeli soldiers were still manning checkpoints at the entrances to Bethlehem, preventing residents from leaving and non-resident Palestinians from entering, and intermittent clashes around nearby Rachel's Tomb disrupted everyday life. With so many Palestinians dying and so many funerals taking place, the town didn't feel much like celebrating, as Palestinians told me when I researched my story.

But it was wonderful for me to see Bethlehem without the jostling crowds. Normally, the queues for the grotto where Jesus' manger once sat would extend all the way out into Manger Square. When I went to visit there was no one there except an old priest praying the rosary. I was lucky to have the place largely to myself.

At a little cafeteria I caught up with Lefteris and his photographer mate, Yannis, who was visiting from Greece and staying with Lefteris for Christmas and New Year. We then made our way to Shepherds' Field, where the procession was supposed to begin. This was where, according to Christian belief, the shepherds watched their flocks and an angel appeared to them to tell them of Jesus' birth.

Being able to visit Bethlehem and see the Church of the Nativity with its tiny grotto as I had that day was a real thrill for me. If I don't believe in anything else, I do believe in Jesus and his ideals. So to have been able to go there and breathe in the same spot, see the place where he was born, was just magical for me. Returning on this day reminded me of that. I was feeling better for it; I was almost beginning to feel that Christmas spirit again, always so freely present in my hometown.

I found Sami, my contact for the story, in the middle of the growing crowd. The procession of people who were recreating the journey had planned a candlelit parade to the Square and the sun was fading quickly. Sami told me to go ahead and speak to anyone I wanted to, as the procession got under way. The people who'd come here to do this were Christians from different churches around the world. They'd followed in the footsteps of the wise men, or the Maji as they were also known, for more than 1000 miles. They'd even travelled through Iraq on their way here.

I approached a tall man with a white beard and white hair, who was wearing long robes and walking with a great staff. He reminded me of Charlton Heston in *The Ten Commandments*. His name was Robin Wainwright and he was from Cold Springs in California. He walked alongside an enormous camel carrying a woman in purple robes and a veil—his wife Nancy. The camels were extraordinary. I'd never seen one up close before and there were at least ten in the group. They had colourful saddlebags on them and stood at least eight feet tall. They had enormous gentle brown eyes and long necks that lolled as they moved. I couldn't stop smiling.

Palestinians from the town began lining the streets to watch the procession, carrying candles in their hands. Wainwright said he had walked the whole way because 'my back doesn't let me ride camels'. They had stayed overnight at Bedouin camps and continued on their way the next day. Among their entourage was a webmaster, who regularly updated their web page, and a water purification expert, who left behind his knowledge in the countries they passed through.

One of the men, a proud-looking Sudanese named Peter Thiet, had had some problems coming into Syria and Israel, but nothing seemed to bother him now. He sat, dressed in bold purple robes, high on his camel and waved regally to the people lining Bethlehem's narrow streets. He spoke to them in Arabic, saying, 'Peace be upon you.'

It was an enchanting evening. Stereo speakers played 'Silent Night' in Arabic and for many of Bethlehem's locals, the procession was a welcome respite from the current tragic events. After I'd tagged along beside Wainwright for a while, I explained I was goggle-eyed at the camels because I'd never ridden one before.

'Well, why don't you ride one now?' he suggested. 'Look, there's one that's free.' He pointed over at a camel without a rider. So I followed him as he walked over to the Bedouin attendant leading the camel and told him I wanted a ride. The attendant made everyone stand back as he alternately hissed and clicked his tongue, getting the animal to bow down on its forelegs until it was kneeling on the ground.

'Okay, get on quickly,' Wainwright said. 'And hold on tight!' he yelled as I scrambled on top. I grabbed at a saddlebag and was nearly thrown forward as the camel stood up, lunging slowly back and forth. It was an incredible feeling and I eventually found my rhythm.

Lefteris, spotting me on the camel, ran over and called out, 'Forget the others, this is the story now!' He started snapping away and I laughed.

It really did begin to feel like Christmas for me and I held on tightly as the giant beast delicately stepped up the slippery steep hills and stairs leading to the illuminated Manger Square.

～∽∾∽～

We spent New Year's Eve at Tzouf nightclub, dancing into the night and early morning. Lefteris and his girlfriend Chryssa came, together with their friends and several others. I held my breath as the clock struck midnight and I looked over at the Old City, its walls lit by a soft yellow glow. I felt glad to be in this incredible old land, which has been loved and wept over by millions of people for thousands of years. I still wasn't anywhere near understanding the how and the why of the place, and I kept vacillating between loving and hating my new life, but at least I felt like I was learning.

It wasn't a good New Year for everyone, though. In the West Bank town of Tulkarem, which was right on the

Israeli border known as the Green Line, a dentist was backing out of his driveway to go to work when his car was shot up by gunmen. He was riddled with bullets. His name was Thabet Thabet and his killing by Israeli soldiers in another 'targeted operation' outraged many. Even among Israelis he was known to be a moderate. He had many Israeli patients and the notion of him being the coordinator of attacks against Israelis was hard for many to reconcile with the quiet, soft-spoken intellectual they knew. The justification Israeli authorities gave was that he was a local Fatah leader, responsible for several attacks. But being a member of Fatah did not automatically make you a member of the militia.

Fatah was the political party that the Palestinian Authority grew from—being a member of it was like being a member of Sinn Fein in Northern Ireland after it became a recognised political party. At first Fatah had been an outlawed revolutionary party, created in exile by Palestinians planning to return triumphant to a Palestinian state. Yasser Arafat had been a terrorist before he sought legitimacy through political dialogue; his movement was behind a number of hijackings and bombings before the Palestine Liberation Organisation, which included Fatah, signed the Oslo Peace Accords with Israel in 1994. After that accord, Arafat was able to return to Palestinian soil and establish the Palestinian Authority. Palestinian members of Fatah returned from the diaspora and became part of the new regime. Palestinians who had never left also joined the party to take part in government.

It was my birthday in the second week of the new year. Lefteris surprised me with 26 red roses, to match my age. I was very touched by the gesture. I got telephone calls and even some cards and gifts in the mail, which was nice. No one sends anything by post these days, so when you get a package it just means so much. My parents were disappointed not to be there with me, but I didn't mind so much after so many people remembered me on the day. That night I went to dinner with a group of friends from the office to Jan's, a restaurant at the Jerusalem Theatre. At Jan's everyone sits on enormous cushions and the menu consists mainly of gratin and soup. The wine was good though.

On 14 January, two Palestinians, one in Gaza City and the other in Nablus, were shot dead by Palestinian firing squads. They'd been accused of collaborating with Israel, of giving Israeli intelligence information on suspected militants—their movements, their friends, their residences, everything needed to locate them and kill them. This information was believed to be the basis of the targeted killings that Israel had undertaken recently. Israeli officials openly admitted that they had had help from the inside when they blew up Palestinian bomb makers in public telephone booths or fired missiles into their cars. The firing squads were the Palestinians' way of warning their people not to cooperate with the enemy. It was treason, the punishment was death.

In Nablus, the family of the man who had been killed by the Israelis, supposedly with the help of the condemned man, were allowed to watch his execution. Mohammed managed to join them and witnessed the whole thing. In Gaza, the shooting took place inside the police compound. Somehow a videotape of the execution got out and Najib, the APTN cameraman in Gaza, fed it to the Jerusalem office. Haitham Hamad, the APTN producer, called me in to come and watch it. He didn't think the figure being executed was actually a man; he thought it was a dummy or something like that. So we watched it carefully. The man had a hood over his head and he was wearing a lot of padding.

'Why's he padded up?' I asked.

'I guess it's so he doesn't make a mess,' Haitham said.

I was becoming inured to the violence I witnessed. By this time my colleagues and I were turning everything into a joke as we couldn't allow ourselves to be moved by what we saw. If we did we'd be incapable of doing our jobs. After four months I was beginning to develop my own mechanisms for dealing with the horror. Just like everyone else, I grabbed at anything I could to lighten the situation. Sometimes though, it wasn't enough.

We could see the tips of the rifles lining the bottom of the screen, pointing at the man who was tied to a pole. When they began firing, we heard a wave of cheers coming from somewhere off-screen. People who'd gathered outside the police compound had heard the shooting and had applauded. Listening to it was bloodcurdling, and I wasn't even there. It sounded like the cries from the lynching of the Israeli soldiers in Ramallah, that call for blood and death no matter how savage the form. The man's body in the video shook and shuddered as it absorbed the impact of the dozens of bullets fired. He continued to shake for moments after the shooting stopped, before finally slumping over. Eventually, he was untied from the pole and carried away by Palestinian police.

The Palestinian Authority received a lot of grief about the executions, especially from the European Union — entry to the EU required dropping the death penalty and the group condemns nations who practise it. Arafat was the only person who could have authorised these executions, so he must have okayed them. It did not make him look good in the eyes of all the diplomats he was trying to keep on his good side.

He promised not to execute any more people, even though at that point there were at least seven others on death row. What would he capitulate to? International opinion or maintaining his domestic political standing?

CHAPTER TEN

end January–6 February 2001

the coalition of political parties that comprised Israel's government was dissolving, despite every attempt by Prime Minister Ehud Barak to resolve the crisis. He'd already lost much support from within his own Labor Party after seemingly offering the Palestinians so much in a peace agreement and being rejected. With the coalition fraying, he called for a prime ministerial vote, to be held on 6 February. In effect, his approach to solving the decades-long crisis was to be decided by the Israeli people. If he won, he could claim vindication and a new mandate to seek a peace process with the Palestinians. The voter's choice was either Barak's subtle diplomacy, or Ariel Sharon's hardline approach of no negotiations, no submission, no giving in until the violence stopped.

Sharon's candidacy surprised a lot of people. The Palestinians called him the Butcher of Beirut because of what had happened in Sabra and Shatila. He was also too hardline for many Israelis. He was a disgraced soldier and politician, yet this lumbering, stern old man was now gaining currency as a possible prime minister. He played the campaign superbly;

barely commenting to the media, preferring to let Barak's mistakes do the talking. The tactic boosted Sharon's position in the polls.

Elizabeth and I travelled to an Israeli–Arab village called Baqa al Gharbieh, on the road to Nazareth, past Haifa. I was to interview some of the locals about who they planned to vote for. Barak had ridden to power the previous time on the Arab vote—95 per cent of them turned out for him after he promised to redress some of the inequities they suffered compared with Israeli citizens. According to the people we spoke to, however, injustice was still rife.

Baqa al Gharbieh's streets were narrow and twisted; the houses haphazard and the power lines perilously unkempt. It looked like a Palestinian town, not an Israeli town, which usually had better local services and construction. It was surreal for me, walking around, seeing shop signs in Hebrew and Arabic, hearing Arabs speak with smatterings of Hebrew. The locals all seemed to end their sentences with *beseder*, Hebrew for 'okay'.

We walked into a tiny grocery store and spoke to a couple of old men sitting in the darkness. They had the same last name: Eghbarieh. Most of the town was descended from the same clan. Mohammed Eghbarieh stood behind the counter, a short, stocky bespectacled man. He said that for him there was no difference between Sharon and Barak, and he might not vote at all. The other man, Taisir Eghbarieh, called them both murderers.

'Sharon killed the Palestinians in Sabra and Shatila, Barak killed them in Jerusalem,' he said. He was referring to the riots in Jerusalem, where five people had been killed in October 2000, at the outset of this intifada. He shrugged, as he stood to leave, lifted the groceries he was carrying in both hands and said it was a hopeless situation.

'They're as bad as each other,' he added.

The Arab-Israelis had their own identity crisis to deal with before they even thought about the Palestinians. There are so many different segments of Palestinian society. There are the refugees from the 1948 and 1967 wars. There are the Palestinians who went overseas—those who were turned out and those who fled—some of them returned in 1994 with the establishment of the Palestinian Authority. Some of these were among Arafat's closest cohorts and were called 'The Tunisians' because they were in Tunis with Arafat after he was exiled from Lebanon. There are also those whose towns were never occupied—those who lived in Ramallah and Nablus and Jericho—and never had to flee because their villages were never taken over. And of course there are also the Arab-Israelis, those who stayed in what became Israel in 1948, and became Israeli citizens.

The Arab-Israelis held Israeli citizenship but unless they were of the Druze faith they could not serve in the army. Many had Palestinian relatives living in the West Bank but because they did not live in a Palestinian area any more, their brethren no longer considered them Palestinians, so they were excluded from identifying with that nationalistic cause. In October 2000, when riots were breaking out all over the West Bank and Gaza, some Arab-Israelis had taken part in local protests as a sign of solidarity with their Palestinian brethren. The riots were brutally quashed by Israeli police. Thirteen young men had been killed and the Arab-Israelis were shocked by the ferocity of the police reaction. Soon after, the government set up a police commission to investigate the events that led to the deaths of the protesters but it wasn't enough. Months later the commission found Barak did not do enough to prevent the violence, but none of the senior officials faced prosecution. The fatalities had fomented resentment among the Arab youth, which only made things worse for locals trying to forge ahead in their own country. It alienated communities and encouraged the extremist elements within the Arab population.

While we were at Baqa al Gharbieh, Elizabeth and I stepped into a shawarma shop to eat while she filed some pictures. Whenever I was working, my attention would inevitably turn to food. I have a huge appetite and Elizabeth barely needed an incentive. We were always on the hunt for good food. We would give our own personal ratings to the different falafel stands and sweet shops we ate at; eventually we had favourite places in most of the Palestinian towns. The shawarma here was different from most of the others we'd tasted elsewhere; you could see the stringy tendons as they sliced the lamb off the spike. The chilli and hummus were so tasty that we kept piling them on the bread.

The owner, Assad Eghbarieh, came up to our table and I invited him to sit down and join us. He was a soft-spoken, obviously educated man. He rang his brother to come over and speak to us as well and soon Shafik, the brother, an accountant, strolled through the doors. Over very powerful black Arabic coffee, they both proceeded to lament the treatment Arabs inside Israel were enduring.

'I feel that we are not citizens of this country, the way they treat us,' Assad said to me, while his brother nodded in agreement. Assad Eghbarieh did not think it likely that Barak would be able to salvage the situation—neither stop the violence nor ensure his political future. There was no possibility, he said, that Barak could present a plan that would be acceptable to Arab-Israelis or to the Palestinians.

January looked like it would end without a peace agreement or any kind of resolution to the conflict, thus hammering the final nail into Barak's political coffin. But there was time for one last gasp at an agreement.

I returned on 18 January 2001 to the Egyptian Red Sea resort of Taba for the negotiations, and this time both sides turned up. I went with Laurie Copans, one of AP's Hebrew-speaking deskers, to cover the story. It was a trip down memory lane for Laurie and a rather fond one too. She had met her husband Danny at Taba in 1995 when the second peace accord was being negotiated. Laurie was our resident fitness guru and champion mountain bike racer; she had a sponsor, and she always came into the office with healthy food prepared. While we all tried to catch the grease from our shawarmas in their wrapping paper, Laurie gobbled plates of lentils and couscous and vegetables, shaming the rest of us. In Taba, Laurie would go for a run along the beach every day, while I could barely drag my weary carcass out of bed. We were complete opposites.

At Taba, Laurie and I got into a routine: I would stay up late chasing the Palestinian negotiators for comments, she would get up early and cover the morning news. We were joined by Salah Nasrawi, an AP Iraqi staffer based in Cairo, as well as by Enric Marti, one of AP's most respected photographers, who was also based in Cairo at the time.

Enric always reminds me of a gangly swan, his long limbs stretching all over the place; chairs and cars were always too small for him. He was tall and his raspy Catalan voice was delightfully sexy. He would blush whenever I pointed this out. It made me laugh that I could make this grown man of 40, one who's chronicled the horrors of Kosovo, Sierra Leone and much of Africa, deadly earthquakes in Turkey and arduous assignments in South America, turn red. He was an inspiration to me because he decided only at the age of 30 that he wanted to take up photography—he'd studied law and worked in his father's business in his native Barcelona before that. Now he was famed for the artistry of his photography. He was also woefully paranoid and a total perfectionist—no one could beat themselves up over a picture more than him. But no one would want Enric to be any other way. He had a few stock phrases, which everyone who knew him would mimic (trying to get his accent right).

'This is bullshit, man,' he'd say about an assignment he'd just covered. Or 'What the fuck?' He'd say that a lot. He came to spend a lot of time in Jerusalem and on Saturdays it was almost routine that he would tease me about my rough appearance in the mornings after a late night.

'You look like shit,' he would say, ruffling my hair. He was the only person who could get away with teasing me like that. When I had the energy to lift myself off the couch in the photos office I would lunge at him, trying to tackle him and embarrass him even more.

The Taba talks were a different ball game for me. Suddenly I was out of the field and in the diplomatic arena with players I'd never seen before or barely knew. So I latched onto my Palestinian colleagues who'd come over for the talks, to see where they would go and whether they would talk to anyone. I eventually got to know most of the negotiators. Saeb Erekat, one of the top Palestinian officials, would find me waiting outside his hotel room trying to get some last-minute comment when he would finally return at 1 a.m. One night he just sighed and shook his head— 'Not now, Jamie'—before turning his key and going in. I met two other senior Palestinian negotiators, Mohammed Dahlan and Nabil Shaath, whose mother was Lebanese and

who took to me immediately. We would stake out the negotiators' rooms in the morning before they went off to the
conference.

Everyone asked about progress. It was the word of the
moment.

'Has there been any progress?'

'Any progress, sir?'

The response was usually about 'gaps' and how wide they
were and whether they were closing or not. We discovered
they were very close to agreeing on territory—what would be
ceded and what would remain, what the Israelis were willing
to return and what the Palestinians were prepared to
stomach. The maps the two sides had were very closely
aligned by the end of the talks but Jerusalem was practically
a non-starter—neither side would budge from their positions.
The Palestinians wanted east Jerusalem as their sover-
eign capital and the Israelis refused. On the refugee issue,
Palestinian and Israeli negotiators would bandy about a
number—150 000 allowed to return and the rest to be
compensated—but there were four million Palestinian
refugees, and neither side would agree to the other's solution
to the situation.

One night I went with my Palestinian colleagues to join
some of the negotiators sitting on a rooftop terrace smoking
waterpipes and drinking hot tea with mint. Dahlan was there
with Erekat, as was Yasser Abed Rabbo, the Palestinian
Information Minister, wearing a woollen cap. They were all
familiar with the journalists, since they'd lived and worked
together for so long. Most of the journalists were from the
Palestinian territories; some of them were even neighbours
with the Palestinian officials and had gone to university with
them. They'd frequent the same restaurants. Everyone knew
about everyone else's movements.

That night, Dahlan wanted to tell everyone a story about Erekat but Erekat insisted he would tell it himself, saying that if he let Dahlan tell it he would exaggerate. So we listened as Erekat told us of a time he was driving back to Jericho, where he lived, from Ramallah, where he'd been working. It was dark and he was without his eye glasses. He was speeding and something suddenly crashed into his car, smashing the windscreen. He got out of the car, cursing and shouting. He'd hit a donkey. He couldn't believe that someone would just let a donkey wander about in the middle of the road in the middle of the night like that. Then he spotted an old lady coming up to the road from a nearby field. He started yelling at her about the donkey while she just stood there looking at him.

'Fine. He's an ass,' he recalled her saying. 'So what does that make you?' Everyone burst out laughing.

Halfway through the talks the Israelis were summoned back to Jerusalem. There'd been another killing. Two Israeli men from Tel Aviv had gone to Tulkarem, a town on the border of the Green Line, to buy some ceramic pots for their sushi restaurant. Either they were entirely naïve about the Palestinians or they were completely ignorant. Everyone used to say that the people of Tel Aviv lived in a bubble because it was so different from the hard, uptight atmosphere in Jerusalem. I always felt like I was on holiday when I spent time in Tel Aviv. These two men were sitting in a restaurant eating hummus when some masked men entered the place, took them away and summarily executed them. I later learnt the circumstances of their deaths first hand, when I met the man who claimed to have killed them, but right now their deaths threatened to derail the talks and everything was put on hold when the Israeli delegation returned to Jerusalem.

As a result, we had a day off. We'd also made an agreement among ourselves not to attempt to bail up the Palestinians because they too were trying to take some time off. We saw Nabil Shaath go for a stroll along the beach while Erekat and Abed Rabbo had lunch by the water. They asked us not to film them or take their picture. One photographer did snap them beachside and he was admonished because they did not want to be seen to be having a good time while the rest of the Palestinian population was in the throes of violent convulsions and funerals. It was frustrating for the negotiators to be here when nothing was going on.

'Palestinians are dying every day,' one of them said. 'If we stop now because of every death we will never get anywhere.'

While I was there I met Ahmed, the nephew of the Palestinian parliamentary speaker, Ahmed Qurei, or Abu Ala, as everyone called him. He was his uncle's personal bodyguard and driver, and was with him all the time. Ahmed helped me out a few times, letting me past other people to have a word with Abu Ala, and holding my tape recorder near his uncle during a media scrum so I wouldn't miss anything he said.

The Israelis returned the next day. On the Saturday they did not move from their hotel, in order to maintain their Sabbath. So the Palestinians went to see them. They were staying at the Princess Hotel in Eilat, on the Israeli side of the border, so we had to cross over to Israel to cover the Saturday talks. It was an incredibly trying day for us. We couldn't even get any coffee in the lobby, because it was the Sabbath and the waitress said she wasn't allowed to operate the machine. I thought I would go out of my mind. No coffee, no food, no moving outside the lobby. I contented myself with chatting up one of the Israeli security guards, who gave me a mini language lesson, teaching me stock Israeli phrases, like *Kama ze*? ('How much is that?'), the numbers and, my favourite at the time, *Ani rutza lishon* ('I want to go to sleep').

I also sat in the lobby with Mark Chisholm, Reuters' outstanding cameraman, as we waited for any delegate to make an appearance. While we swapped armchairs and paced up and down the large hall, we covered a range of subjects in talks of our own. I told him that since my arrival in Israel I had not failed to notice how well-endowed Israeli women were. No matter how thin they were, virtually all of them had a spectacular cleavage. Mark agreed. He turned to his soundman Rami, an Israeli, to ask him why it was that Israeli women had such big breasts. Rami just smiled and said: 'It's the land of milk and honey, mate.' We couldn't argue with that statement—it seemed pretty plausible from where we were sitting.

The summit was close to an end but there were no indications that a resolution was near. Pressure was mounting and expectations from both sides—not to mention the rest of the world—was overwhelming. It was crunch time on many levels. This summit was suppose to save Barak's neck and get him re-elected. It was supposed to put an end to the fighting and stop more people from dying. It was supposed to push the Israeli–Palestinian conflict further towards resolution. Everyone was waiting for something positive to come out of it. Everyone, all over the world, was watching in anticipation. Even my parents called from Australia to tell *me* about it.

At one point, when Abu Ala addressed reporters, I stood right next to him, holding out my recorder. All the cameramen later told me that I was in every frame, so I rang my parents and told them to watch CNN in case they showed me. They did, quite often, and my parents taped it. It was quite an emotional moment for them, seeing me on television. They hadn't seen my face since September.

On the final day, Sunday, there was a joint declaration

but no agreement, no undertakings; just a statement. It was a bitter disappointment. Accusations immediately flew about who was to blame, who didn't give in and who walked away in the end. It was a free-for-all. Blame was dished out and the mood was generally one of despair. Some said Arafat had again refused to give Barak an agreement. Barak would not capitulate on important issues, said others. The positions of both sides only became clearer years after; the Israelis later said it was too close to the elections to risk such an undertaking, while the Palestinians blamed the Israelis for refusing to compromise on key issues. We returned to Jerusalem.

The following Saturday was quiet and rainy. I was sitting in the office when Karin asked me to go with Laurent to cover a Labor Party rally Barak was attending in Kiryat Shemona, on the border with Lebanon. I had a cold but I agreed to go, mainly because I disliked being in the office. Given a choice between being in the field and being in the office, there was never any contest.

We travelled to Tel Aviv, where many of the Laborites would be starting their procession to Kiryat Shemona, along the No. 1 highway that stretches from one end of Israel to the other. Everywhere there were blue-and-white streamers, the colours of the Labor Party, and posters were stuck on the cars in the car park as they got ready to travel to the north. The party's supporters were planning to drive up in a convoy—a flutter of blue and white blurring past motorists along the length of the country. They seemed so optimistic when I spoke to them. The latest polls—the ones showing Barak slipping and destined to lose—were ignored.

As we were driving, Laurent decided he wanted to zip ahead and climb onto a footbridge to photograph the travelling convoy as it approached. He hit the accelerator, came to a footbridge and jumped out, asking me to take the wheel. I slid over, scattering Kleenex everywhere, and waited for Laurent to take the pictures. Then he came running back down, wanting me to speed ahead to the next footbridge, dissatisfied with what he'd shot so far. I hit the accelerator and we were off. We stopped and sped several times after that. Then Laurent wanted to shoot while we were travelling. I was driving at between 100 and 110 kilometres per hour. At one point Laurent, slumped in his seat, turned and looked at me and said, in his heavy French accent, 'Better to be in clashes in Ramallah zen in a car wiz a woman driver.' At that point I pulled over and told him to drive. As far as he was concerned, I was too slow.

When we arrived at Kiryat Shemona, I was unexpectedly moved to see that we were right on the border with Lebanon. It was so weird for me to be so near, yet so far from a country I knew well. The high, dark green mountains reminded me of my father's eldest sister Marie, who lived in Hiyata, a mountain village in Lebanon. We used to look down from her terrace and see fog circling the mountains. It was fresh and clean; the air practically froze in your throat as you inhaled. One time we were on our way to visit her and her husband with one of my uncles and his family. We stopped at a shop to buy some extra groceries but once they were stashed into the car, along with my cousins, there was no room for anyone else. Christine, my younger sister, and I climbed into the boot of the sedan while everyone else crammed into the car. She and I laughed as we rolled around in the back as the car lurched up the mountain for the remainder of the trip.

Kiryat Shemona was a town that attracted climbers and tourists. In the winter people would come to ski, though the snowfall was not too dramatic. I felt as though, if I shouted loud enough, people on the other side—in Lebanon—would be able to hear me. It was drizzling and cold and I was feeling very poorly with the flu by this point. I struggled to stay awake as we sat in a café awaiting the rally.

Kiryat Shemona was a Labor-friendly town. Many people there felt indebted to Barak for agreeing to withdraw from Lebanon in May 2000. Up to that time the constant rain of wayward Katyusha rockets from the Hezbollah across the border had forced Israelis into underground shelters. The bombs were so erratic no one knew where they would land. It had created hardships for people living here on the front line.

We shuffled past security and into the hall where Barak would address the crowd. When he entered the room, young Labor members charged towards him, embracing him and cheering wildly. The cheering and whooping lasted until he reached the podium and waved his hands in the air, smiling as widely as he could. In this corner of the country Barak seemed like a sure thing. Everyone was talking about victory.

On polling day, 6 February 2001, Elizabeth and I went to see how the Arab-Israeli towns would vote. We started in a tiny village called Jaljulya in central Israel, where the streets were empty and we struggled to find anyone to interview, let alone a prospective voter. It appeared the Arabs had boycotted this election en masse, as they said they would. It did not bode well for Barak. I stopped some people at the local school to ask who they voted for but they refused to say. At the polling station I asked how many people had come to vote and the man sitting behind the desk said he'd barely seen anyone all day.

We travelled up to Baqa al Gharbieh, to see what was happening there. The relatives of the youths shot in the October riots were calling on everyone in the different towns in that area to boycott the elections completely. They drove slowly in long motorcades with black flags, while a voice from a loudspeaker mounted on one of the cars beseeched their fellow Israeli-Arab citizens to remember the fallen youths and to send a message to Barak that they as a part of the population wouldn't be ignored.

I was driving while Elizabeth took pictures. She would hop out and run and take some photos, then run and catch up with me and we would continue on. At one point I got so distracted that I accidentally bumped the car in front of me. Wide-eyed, I poked my head out the window and said, 'Sorry,' over and over to the driver, who got out of his car and started waving his arms around wildly, complaining I'd damaged his car. I said I was sorry and people standing on the footpath looked at his car and told him to stop being so dramatic.

'There's nothing there!'

'Stop complaining!' they said, laughing him into silence.

As everyone had predicted, Sharon won the election. There was an overwhelming sense of pessimism and gloom among the journos. There was also an almost immediate recognition that an era had ended and the peace process was unlikely to be revisited in the near future. In Israel there was now a hawk in office and in Washington there was a new president, George W. Bush, who at this time was disengaged from world affairs and wanting to return the United States' focus inward.

It was like a giant 'pause' button had been pressed.

PART TWO

an end brings
new beginnings

CHAPTER ELEVEN

Ramallah
14 November 2004

omeone's going to die today, I couldn't stop thinking. That
much was obvious. The crowd that had begun the day
outside the Muqataa was now inside and Arafat's
body would be arriving any minute. I was watching from a
building overlooking the Palestinian Authority compound,
not daring to get closer. Mohammed Daraghmeh was in there
somewhere; the only thing I'd get that he wouldn't was
endless groping. We'd been waiting since morning, it was
now past noon and the helicopters were due any moment.
We waited and watched.

The crowd was growing by the minute, filling the grounds
that had been hurriedly cleared and prepared overnight for
the funeral. Bulldozers had worked to clear the area, digging
up dirt to make a grave of marble and sand for the Palestinian leader, who had died in France the day before. Into the
early hours of the morning a band had played, marching up
and down the helipad while they practised.

In February 2003, I had left Jerusalem and returned to Sydney. I needed to go home. I took a posting at the AP Sydney bureau and covered stories in my hometown. I watched my elder sister, Maria, get married. Another friend also tied the knot and I'd been so happy to be there to take part. That was the biggest reason for my return to Australia: to get away from the madness and just absorb normal life for a change. I needed to reconnect with people whose lives didn't revolve around a story, especially one so linked to death and sadness. Everyone in Sydney marvelled at my cynicism. I was too hard and world weary. I needed to know softness again.

Much as I enjoyed being at home, I had still felt the pull of covering bigger stories. In 2003 and 2004 I spent two summers in Baghdad. I kept wondering, *Am I forever going to be part of the Middle East, a place I so desperately wanted to escape as a child? Or Am I now fully programmed to be a foreign correspondent; to only ever really came alive in war zones?* I had to face the fact that, as I sat there restlessly at my desk in beautiful sunny Sydney after the war erupted in Iraq, I wanted to be there. Life was too easy at home, people there didn't really know what it was to suffer. Paradoxically, I couldn't have been happier. I never wanted Australia to be anything like the places I'd been to and I never wanted Australians to know the fear and frustration of living in a place where life was fragile and uncertain.

While I was in Baghdad in August 2003, I sat in the AP photos office at al Hamra Hotel in Baghdad and watched as television news reported that Ismail Abu Shanab had been killed in a rocket attack. I was shocked. I well remembered the quietly spoken Hamas leader, whom I had interviewed in his house in a shanty neighbourhood of Gaza. I remembered his little girl, Hiba, who would interrupt our talks.

I wondered what everyone would tell her when she asked for her father. I tried to understand why Israel would kill this man while other leaders like Sheik Ahmed Yassin and Abdel Aziz al-Rantisi remained alive. They were far more radical than he was—did they want to kill everyone so there was absolutely no one to talk to? But Hamas was always dedicated to the destruction of Israel.

Only months later, both Yassin and al-Rantisi were killed; one soon after the other. Marwan Barghouti was jailed and convicted by Israel for organising deadly attacks against Israelis and a Greek monk. He is in jail for a minimum of five life sentences. *What will become of him?* I wonder. I managed to follow this story from Australia, on the other side of the world; and it continued to grip me. In fact, it never left me and I'd heard from others that, once you have lived in the Middle East and shared in its history, it will always be a part of you.

The pull I felt to be in Ramallah for Arafat's funeral was irresistible. The idea of watching it on television in Sydney, and not being part of it, was wrenching. I volunteered to make the journey and then a call came from New York in the middle of the night: 'First plane out'. I could barely conceal my excitement, even though everyone else at home was completely dismayed at my going. I couldn't help it. I realised that I had to be here, that this was a part of me, who I had become. I could deny it no longer.

Arafat was flown out from his compound by helicopter on 29 October amid rumours about the cause of his sickness. At first I couldn't believe he was as sick as doctors were suggesting. He was a fit man. He exercised every day, he walked on a treadmill for half an hour and he ate well. He was fitter than Sharon, who was older and fatter and seemed like a walking advertisement for bad cholesterol.

I arrived in Ramallah on 8 November and waited outside his compound for news on his condition, along with the rest of the world's media. I saw friends again, many of whom had also returned for the funeral. I'd lost weight they said, my hair was darker, and the main question thrown at me: 'What? Still not married?'

My love life was still its own disaster zone. I hadn't been able to have a proper relationship since that last commitment in Singapore in 2000. I was hopeless. But I knew myself better now, of course. I was turning 30 and feeling better about my place in the world, what I wanted to do and where I wanted to go. And I had the love of my family and friends, who remained with me in spite of everything and because of everything.

I was glad to be back in the Holy Land. I needed to be back here to know if it was just me who had been so affected by the circumstances that faced me when I first arrived, all those years ago, or if it had hit others too. And I needed a conclusion to this story.

CHAPTER 12

I knew that, like any other Western woman in my situation in the Middle East, I was an object of curiosity. By merely doing my job, I was breaking most of their social codes. Palestinian women and men that I met couldn't understand how my father—since I wasn't married, they believed he was responsible for me—would allow me to live abroad by myself and do such a dangerous job. My assurances that he was generally supportive of my decisions rattled their sense of a woman's place in the world. Also, I wasn't married—another thing about my life that puzzled many. There were moments when my being so different was jarringly clear, most especially when I worked in the Gaza Strip.

I was used to being one of the few women to be seen out and about in Gaza without a headscarf. Whenever I saw another unveiled female, my interest was always piqued. Someone told me the influence of Hamas was so strong there that girls as young as eight years old were donning headscarves and the few Palestinian Christians who lived there felt intimidated by the custom. I couldn't cross the street without stopping traffic. Motorists would lean on their horns when I tried to cross the road, my hair hanging free, wearing jeans but with my arms covered by long-sleeved shirts or a jacket. It was obvious I wasn't from around Gaza, so I felt I couldn't pretend to blend in. That, I believed, would have been more offensive.

During one stint there in 2001, I was assigned to write a feature on Palestinian women. I asked Ibrahim Barzak, our local Palestinian reporter, where I could go to speak to some professional women. Ibrahim said I wouldn't find a female writer, or driving instructor or businesswoman in Gaza. That surprised me. I knew conditions were difficult for women, Western or otherwise. The female photographers who worked there seemed to take it for granted that, whenever they covered a protest or demonstration, some wandering Palestinian hands would invariably feel them up.

Aiman, the AP driver, and I taught Elizabeth a couple of words in Arabic to say to anyone who tried to grab her. The one that always seemed to work best was *haram*, which means 'forbidden' in Arabic. Alcohol was *haram* in Islam, and even looking at women, let alone touching them, was frowned upon. The most perplexing thing for me was that usually the ones doing all the groping were little boys. Many of them were barely twelve yet they were trying to grab your bottom. What had they been told about Western women?

Once Elizabeth had succeeded in embarrassing one young boy, who'd grabbed her as he was passing by. She turned and grabbed his hand and began yelling *'Haram! Haram!'*, shaking his arm. Her cries set off a nearby group of boys, who then started hitting the boy, shouting *'Haram!'* as they did so.

For a while I enjoyed telling friends that I'd only ever been felt up once, and that had been at the scene of a car bomb—

in an ultra-Orthodox Jewish-Israeli neighbourhood. It was one of the first car bombings I'd witnessed. I had arrived in Mea Shearim as the car was smouldering on the side of a street, up against a wall. There were signs everywhere in neighbourhoods such as this one, warning visitors to cover themselves before entering.

'Do not offend the modesty of our women and children', the signs read. 'Wear long sleeves and cover yourselves completely'. Just the same sort of dress code I'd had to abide by when I'd been in Gaza.

I wondered at the men and women who lived there and how they could tolerate their heavy clothing in the Middle Eastern heat. It may have been appropriate for Poland or Russia, but the Judean desert was less than an hour's drive from Jerusalem. Over the men's shirts and waistcoats were heavy black jackets, long trousers and socks. It was stifling just looking at them.

At the bomb site the police had set up a cordon and were pushing the crowd back. The street was full of black-hatted men and youths who surged against the cordon. I was in the unhappy position of being at the front of the crowd, and I pleaded with the police officer near me to let me through the barrier. It was too crowded, but he was unmoved. I was about to protest again when I felt a hand cup my bottom, none too subtly, and give it a firm squeeze. I spun around, enraged, and pushing the crowd away from me I yelled, 'Fuck off!'

The men in front of me gasped in unison and stepped back. Then some of them turned their backs on me while the others began spitting at me. I couldn't stop swearing, I was so angry.

'Fuck you! Fuck you! You fucking assholes!' I was wildly outnumbered. There were about 200 of them and only one of me. I really shouldn't have been antagonising them, I realised, but then I wasn't thinking straight. I just wanted to get out of there. I could feel my claustrophobia beginning to set in. I tried to get through the throng, but they were unyielding. If I wasn't going to get any help from them, I thought, *I will move you myself.* So I did.

I forced my way through a maze of skinny men with side-locks and black hats, who either spat at me or turned their backs on me. I was too angry and frustrated to think about why they were doing what they were doing. They were so skinny and I was bigger than most of them. I pushed one after the other aside until I finally got through the mass and was able to breathe again.

I would bring up this anecdote whenever colleagues complained about being molested by Palestinian crowds. For me, it was only another way of showing that the so-called differences between the two people were really not that great.

‿❧‿

In my quest to find more working women in Gaza, Elizabeth and I went to a sewing factory at the Beach Refugee Camp, one of the many refugee camps within the Gaza Strip. We stepped into a room filled with rows of women at small desks, hunched over sewing machines. The fluorescent ceiling lights flickered and I wondered how they focused on the small stitching under such bad lighting. We looked around to see what they were working on. A young boy came into the room carrying a bundle of jeans with cotton threads still lined through them. Some of the women were sewing together bright yellow halterneck tops — 'For the women in Israel,' they said to me, giggling.

'Look at what the Israelis wear,' said one woman who was covered from head to toe. I couldn't help laughing at the irony.

One of the women was the same age I was at the time, 26. Her name was Loubna and she had a wide smile framed by her headscarf. She said she had wanted to learn English while at school, but she left to be married at eighteen.

'What does your husband do?' I asked her.

'I don't have a husband,' she said with a wave of her hand. 'I'm a divorcee.'

'Really?' I asked. I was intrigued. I'd not met a divorced Palestinian woman before. If they existed, they were always well hidden, especially in a society as conservative as Gaza. There was such a social stigma attached to divorce; it stained the woman as well as her family. I had to find out more, so I took Loubna's phone number and told her I would like to see her again. She happily agreed.

My next stop for this assignment was at a high school run by the United Nations Refugee and Welfare Agency. It was a girls' school in Beach Camp. Elizabeth and I were led into the library and soon after a group of girls, aged about fourteen or fifteen, filed silently into the room and sat timidly around a large table with me. The UN man who organised the meeting sat near me, along with a male teacher. I was conscious of their presence and didn't want it to inhibit the girls, so I asked them to leave. Once they did, the girls immediately relaxed.

Talking with them was a lot of fun. They all spoke fluent English and had many questions for Elizabeth and me, about our jobs, our lifestyle, and the countries we came from. Coincidentally, many of the girls were preparing for a geography exam on Australia later that afternoon. I asked them about their dreams for the future. They were all studying hard to win one of the few scholarships the Palestinian Authority offered to bright students. For some it would be their only chance to make a real change in their lives.

It was fascinating talking to these girls. One strong-willed girl said her father was totally supportive of her improving and getting an education and moving forward with her life. Another admitted that, if she didn't get the scholarship, the family's money would go to supporting her brother and his future.

'A girl can always get married,' she said.

Despite their ambitions, the girls said they would never go against their parents' wishes. They admitted that being girls in a traditional Muslim society could cost them their dreams, particularly those who come from large families. They said the intifada was their greatest obstacle to continuing their education. The violence had increased the number of un-employed and broken the fragile Palestinian economy. Whatever slim opportunities there were before the violence, they had sharply dwindled and would continue to decline as they progressed through school.

One girl wanted to be a lawyer, another a psychologist. They all wanted to travel and they all wanted to return to Gaza and give something back. They took my breath away. One girl didn't wear a headscarf, and one said she wore one only when she left the house.

'Are you a Muslim?' one asked me.

'No,' I replied.

'Why not? You should become a Muslim. Everyone should be Muslim,' she said.

When I asked why, she replied, 'Because Islam is the best religion.' I didn't want to point out that Islam—or, at least, the version of Islam they were growing up with—would prevent them from being everything they wanted to be.

They asked how we could live away from our families, doing what we do. Weren't we afraid? It was our turn to shake our heads and dismiss the idea. Not really, we both said.

'You are very strong,' they said to us. Elizabeth and I just looked at each other and turned to them and said, 'No, you are the strong ones.' They really were.

Each afternoon they would leave the cheerful rooms of their schools, where the walls were covered with hand drawings and event notices, for the dreariness of the camps. Scuffing their shoes in the sand they would walk home, where they would make for the kitchen and help their mothers look after their brothers and fathers. They'd do the laundry, cook, carry groceries and stay indoors and out of view when visitors came over. They'd lose the battle for the television remote control and be ignored at the dinner table. They would marry the person their father told them to marry. They would never disobey their parents. They would try to make the best of their lot in life, no matter what it was.

The very idea made me choke. I couldn't cope with that kind of powerlessness. I had begun to recognise that I was something of a control freak; the minute anyone tried to exert influence over the way I lived or thought or worked, I would react forcefully. I could never live like these girls. I'd rebelled against my own father for years before I finally broke away and travelled to Singapore. I always knew I would get out. I believed that, even if my circumstances had been different, there was no way I could submit, just yield like that and allow someone else to control my destiny. These girls would have to have enormous reservoirs of inner strength to endure the possibility that their hopes and dreams would never come to fruition. That was something I knew I did not possess. I wanted to stay and talk to them all afternoon.

◦≈≈◦

I visited Loubna at her parents' home and I sat with her and her feisty mother as she talked about her short-lived marriage. She talked as we went through her wedding album, looking at the pictures.

'I had no idea what I was doing,' she said. 'To me, I was just wearing a pretty dress and going to a party.' There were no photos of her husband, just an empty, cut-out silhouette of where he had been in many of the pictures.

'I've cut him out of my life,' she said, so much so, I couldn't even get his name out of her. Like many others, hers was an arranged marriage. She'd never even met her husband until their wedding day. She was eighteen and they were strangers, but when they married, she said she loved him.

'I wouldn't even let him do up his own shoelaces,' she said. 'I looked after him in every way. There was nothing he did, I did everything for him.'

After two years of marriage, Loubna still hadn't conceived a child. She learnt that her husband had been married before, and his mother had forced him to divorce his first wife because that union had also failed to produce children. Then the first wife's father died and Loubna's husband allowed the first wife to move back in with them, ostensibly to ease the load she placed on her own family. Loubna was 20 by this time.

'I went from living with my husband to living in a room out in the back,' Loubna said. 'I had to argue with this woman over the days I would get to sleep with my own husband!' Even so many years later, she still seemed incredulous that it had turned out this way. She said she persisted because she loved him. Then came the kicker. His mother brought him another bride. Muslim men can take up to four wives, provided they can meet all their needs equally. When wife number three arrived, it was the last straw for Loubna.

'She should have left him years ago!' yelled her mother, a fat, jolly woman. As we spoke, Loubna sat cross-legged on the floor, pounding flour and salt with water into a dough. I'd told her I loved bread when it was cooked on a 'sage'—the dough is spread thinly over a cushion, then the cushion is used to place the dough over a hot plate over a fire until it is brown and crispy—so she was determined to make me some. Apparently her ex-husband still had no heirs, something that set off Loubna's mother again.

'She should have checked out her own son before she even looked at my daughter!' she yelled, and then laughed. We all laughed. I was fascinated by Loubna's story, to hear about her customs and culture. I wondered whether Loubna was an outcast in her society. She dismissed the idea when I asked her. She said that, since her family had stood by her unquestioningly, their acquaintances didn't have a choice. She had no hope of ever going back to school, or of finishing learning English, because she said she was now too old. But she still wanted to become a nurse one day. For now, she worked; the US$6 per day she made as a seamstress went straight to her family and her father gave her an allowance to pay for transport or anything else she might want. It was sad to see her so enthusiastic and ambitious, then to look at her surroundings and think that this was all she might ever be. I wanted more for her.

Aiman, who had driven me there, could not sit with us women as we talked, as Loubna's family was Bedouin, and their customs dictated a separation of men and women — after all, Loubna had only met her husband on their wedding day. Her father took him out to a tent in the backyard. The old man even lit a fire for him — in the stifling Gaza heat, inside the tent. When I met up with him later, Aiman reeked of smoke, something I laughed about all the way back to the office.

⌒⌒

Elizabeth often accompanied me as I also interviewed female politicians and female doctors for the story. By the time I neared the end of the assignment I thought I'd seen it all. That was before I met Soubhiyeh.

She greeted us at the door of her tiny abode, squeezed into a stack of concrete cubes in a refugee camp. I stepped into the dark, cement hole that was her living room and looked around. The place was damp and small, and to me it felt like the concrete walls were closing in. I looked at her, heavily pregnant and lifting a young child over her swollen belly onto her hip. Her hair was as dirty as that of her seven children. I couldn't believe anyone could live like this. She was just 32 and she swore the eighth child would be her last.

I looked over at her husband and her father-in-law, sitting on plastic chairs in the middle of the squalid room, listening to our conversation. There was another room that looked like a closet, stacked with rolled-up mattresses where she said she slept with most of the children. There was no bathroom or kitchen. There was a hot water tank and a camping stove in another dent in the living room wall. She said one of her children had burnt himself with hot oil because she was cooking on the stove in the middle of the room. A small boy came up to her and buried his scarred face into her belly as she touched his head lightly.

I didn't want to stay long. She was asking me where I came from, what I was doing, where I lived. I didn't want to tell her a thing. I couldn't; I felt so bad looking at her, trying not to be disgusted by her situation. I didn't want her to envy me or feel sad about her own prospects. She said that once the child she was carrying was born and was a bit older, she would do a sewing course or learn a trade so she could work and have more of a life. She said she was one of many girls in her family and her parents decided to marry them off to avoid looking after them any longer.

Maybe I'd been too sheltered and I certainly felt incredibly naive. It seemed that for every jewellery-flashing, BMW-driving rich Palestinian housewife there were 500 other women whose circumstances were horrible. Poor women like Soubhiyeh lived in a society where they were bartered as merchandise and bore children and prepared food. They couldn't have an opinion, an education, a social life outside their neighbourhood. How do you explain to someone in this sort of situation that you live in a country on the other side of the world, when they haven't even been outside of the Gaza Strip? As I tried to understand, I often did impart my own experiences and opinions to the people I came in contact with. Sometimes I just provided the entertainment.

I remember in the summer of 2001, when I was covering a demonstration in Gaza City with some other female journalists, we were passing one of the legislative buildings and I felt a sharp stab of pain in my side, right underneath my arm. I flinched and grabbed at my side, flicking a hornet onto the ground.

'Oh no, you should go to the hospital straightaway. You might be allergic,' cried Dominique, one of the reporters with me. It wasn't long before the pain sunk in.

'Ouch, ouch, OUCH!' I yelled. By some miracle Aiman pulled up alongside me and I ran towards him.

'To Shifa, Aiman, and hurry up!' I screamed.

I had always believed that I would be admitted into the emergency ward of Al-Shifa Hospital in Gaza City, but I had thought it would be for something like a bullet wound, or from being hit by a stone, nothing as embarrassing as a hornet sting. Since I didn't even know the Arabic word for the bloody creature, I was trying to describe it to Aiman as he sped to the hospital.

'It's like a bee, only much, much bigger,' I emphasised, grabbing my side in agony.

'Ahhh, okay,' he said, trying not to laugh.

'This isn't funny, Aiman,' I snapped, red-faced. 'This is really painful.'

While I could see the funny side, I was more humiliated than anything else and his laughter wasn't helping.

I ran into the emergency section of the hospital, a place where I'd previously seen many dead bodies being carted past angry sweating crowds. I began to yell. I started to take my top off because the hornet had stung me right under my arm, along my rib cage. I was wearing a bra underneath so it wasn't like I would be completely naked. But all the doctors began shouting, '*La! La!*'—'No! No!'—to stop me from stripping there and then. I had to remind myself this was a Muslim society. One of them led me to a hospital bed and pulled the curtain across to hide me from view. A female nurse came and watched as was the custom.

I finally got to yank off my top and pointed to the bite, which was dark red with a small circle of pink where the sting was spreading. The modesty of the bra I was wearing that day did nothing to deflect the doctor's discomfort. Embarrassed, he held the stethoscope towards me, but looked in another direction. *I don't believe this*, I thought. I grabbed the thing and stuck it on my chest and took a few deep breaths.

'Okay, okay,' he said, and walked out. I was in so much pain and I'd run out of patience. The nurse who had also walked out with the doctor returned and said she had to give me a shot.

'Okay,' I said and put my top back on. I noticed she looked uncomfortable.

'What is it?' I asked.

'You have to turn around,' she said. I stood up, turned around and waited. I looked back at her, my face contorted, trying to stifle screams, and asked, 'What is it?'

'You have to take off your pants,' she said, fidgeting.

'My pants?' I asked. Then it sunk in. I pulled my underwear down and braced for the needle.

'There's two,' she said.

'Okay, okay, just do it,' I answered.

Then I heard her say in Arabic, 'In the name of God the merciful,' before plunging a needle into each of my butt cheeks.

When we emerged from behind the curtain, the doctor told me to go straight back to my hotel because I was going to pass out. And I did, once I was back in my hotel room. When I woke up all I saw were flowers which several people had sent me, as well as some get-well cards. One of the hotel staff had snuck in while I was asleep to place them there for me to see when I re-emerged. I was so embarrassed. I had never expected my only hospital visit in Gaza would be for something as paltry and undignified as a hornet sting.

Gaza illuminated the Muslim world and its traditions for me. I was obliged to speak Arabic most of the time I was there, so my command of that language really began to improve, and I liked to mingle with locals, even though sometimes they were uncomfortable mingling with me. I know I frustrated Aiman no end. During a stint there in 2002, one of my friends from Jakarta, photographer Charlie Dharapak, came to spend a month. It was right before his wedding and it was great to see him and hang out. One of the stories we worked on was how the Gazans felt about Arafat's confinement—he'd been Ramallah-bound since December 2001 and Sharon said he wouldn't be allowed to move back to Gaza until those who'd assassinated Israeli cabinet minister Rehavam Zeevi were handed over. Arafat held firm, but so did Sharon. No matter the efforts of the US, the UN and other envoys to break the stalemate, nothing changed.

I wanted to go to a coffee shop where a lot of Fatah people hung out, to see how Arafat's cohorts were coping with the fact that he wouldn't be coming back to Gaza anytime soon. Aiman took us to a smoky café full of old men playing backgammon and cards, puffing on waterpipes and drinking tea with cardamom. I really liked the atmosphere as soon as we walked in so we ordered coffees and sat down. Aiman looked almost bashful when our coffees arrived.

'What's wrong with you?' I cajoled, nudging him across the table.

'My dear, Jamie,' he said. 'Look around you—this is a coffee shop for men. They come here to escape their wives.' I translated for Charlie and we both started laughing.

'Good!' I said to Aiman. 'If you don't mind, please ask one of these gentlemen if he'd like to have a conversation with me.' Sighing loudly, he got up and asked around. After we spoke to some of the men briefly, who said that they weren't really surprised Israel hadn't allowed Arafat to return, and that his absence was being felt here in the Strip, we left.

Aiman and I got along well. I was easier to deal with because of my background, I guess, than photographers or reporters who weren't from the Middle East and were still learning its culture. He was responsible for anyone who came to Gaza to work. He was the bodyguard, the fixer, the translator. That I understood Arabs and Arabic made it easier for him to negotiate anything, from clearing a path through a debris-filled bomb site to walking into a funeral house and getting some quotes for a story. It never ceased to surprise me that, whenever I walked into a house or office or spoke with people in the field, I was immediately taken in as one of them once they discovered my Lebanese roots.

'All Arabs are brothers,' they used to say.

Charlie and I went to Aiman's house as his family prepared to celebrate the Muslim feast of *Eid al-Adha*. Charlie wanted to photograph the proceedings and, since I'd not witnessed much of the ritual before, I agreed to go too. Aiman and his brother were sharing a goat for the feast. I don't know what I was expecting. I somehow thought the animal would already be dead and they'd be chopping it up like you'd see a butcher do. I didn't think it would be alive and all white and fluffy, as the goat Aiman led into the front courtyard of his house was. I couldn't watch. It reminded me of the only other time in my life I'd seen an animal slaughtered.

At the tiny village where we'd lived in Lebanon my sisters and I were standing on the balcony watching some of the village kids lead a cow to the butchers across the road from our building. To our horror, the butchers looped a rope around each of the cow's legs until it was dangling upside down. Then they slit it open down the belly and started carving it up. It was still alive until they sliced its throat. That memory was potent in my mind as I watched the white goat in Aiman's courtyard flail helplessly and uselessly on the ground, its hooves spreading its dark blood all over the tiles. I went inside with Aiman's wife and sister-in-law.

We sat in the living room and talked; I didn't even want to pretend that I wasn't disturbed by the scene outside. The women told me they had five children each, so between them, Aiman and his brother had ten children. I was amazed; their wives were my age.

'Why aren't you married yet?' they asked me.

'Oh, it's too soon,' I answered, then laughed as I realised that they'd both been married for years. Luckily they laughed too.

It was hard to know if my Western views offended them or not. Sometimes I felt like I was flaunting my independence in such women's faces or I was coming across as arrogant because of how I lived and especially because their husbands worked for me.

Here I was, the same age but independent and working away from home and family; and the relationship I had with their husbands was on a completely different level from theirs. Aiman had to be there whenever I rang, day or night, late or early. He would often have to leave them to come and help me. It was a delicate line to walk sometimes.

Aiman used to joke that Elizabeth was his second wife. Once when we were driving in Gaza City he said to me, 'You know Jamie, you're getting old. If you turn 30 and you still haven't gotten married, I'll marry you.' Looking at me and winking he reminded me, 'You know, I'm allowed to have four.'

I ingested this offer with a smile.

'Sure,' I said, staring ahead at the road and smiling. 'That sounds fine, as long as I can have four too.'

'But you can't!' Aiman exclaimed. 'That doesn't work!'

I played dumb and carried on.

'Why not? If you can have four, I should be able to have four too. What's the problem?'

Aiman jerked back and forth in his seat, leaning over the steering wheel as he tried to make his point.

'It doesn't work like that.'

I kept pushing.

'But why not?'

'Because . . . because . . .' He didn't want to say.

'Tell me why,' I pressed.

'Because, if a man is married to four women and one of the women gets pregnant, they all know who the father is, because there's only one man.'

'Well, so what?' I asked. 'If a woman has four husbands and she gets pregnant by one of them, at least it's one of her husbands who is the father.'

'No! It doesn't work like that!' he said, shaking his head.

'Well I don't know why it would be fine for the man but not for the woman to be married to four different people,' I said. It really didn't make any sense to me and I wasn't going to accept what I saw as a blatant double standard. To me, Muslim women always seemed to get the rough end of the stick.

CHAPTER THIRTEEN

before the terrorist attacks of September 11, 2001 and the wars in Iraq and Afghanistan, there were suicide bombings in Israel. We all knew about them; we'd already seen their toll. The Palestinians had been using them to hit at the Israelis for years. It had been Hamas' weapon of choice during the early 1990s and when the second intifada of 2000 erupted they vowed to start up the tactic again.

The first suicide bombing I covered was in March 2001, just two days before I was due to fly home to Sydney—my first trip back since leaving Singapore for Jerusalem, so at the time I was anxious to get home. Elizabeth and I were driving out of Jerusalem towards Ramallah to meet Marwan Barghouti, with whom we'd lined up an interview. We had stopped at the traffic lights under the bridge that leads to Pisgaat Zeev, a Jewish settlement on the outskirts of Jerusalem—an area the locals called French Hill—when suddenly the wails of siren upon siren filled the air. Normally impatient road warriors didn't even honk their horns, everyone just stopped moving to allow a border police Jeep to careen past down the hill.

Elizabeth grabbed her cameras, jumped out of the car and slammed the door behind her.

'Drive,' she shouted back at me as she started running. I climbed into the driver's seat and pulled the car over onto the median strip, then got out and ran down the hill after her.

Fifty metres away, I saw a bus. Its back window had been shot out and rimmed in black. The bus was wedged halfway up the hill. This image confronted me as I bounded towards the bus. I kept running, looking only at the bus, not noticing the Israeli policeman who stepped in my path and seized both my shoulders and said *'Lo, hamouda,'* which meant 'No, cutie', and firmly stopped me.

'But I have to get over there,' I told him, pointing at the bus. 'I'm a journalist. I have to go there,' I said, jumping up and down, saying *'Etonayit'*, the Hebrew word for 'journalist', over and over. He was unmoved. In the middle of arguing with him something tugged at the corner of my left eye. I turned to look and, on the footpath, I saw a large dark purple blob of what I quickly realised was someone's insides. I sank out of the policeman's grip, nodding.

'Okay, okay, I won't go. I'm already far enough.'

I started shaking as the full extent of what I was witnessing sank in. I rang the office and described the scene to them: the shattered glass; the bloodied passengers carried away to ambulances, some screaming, some quiet, still in shock; the smell of newly extinguished fire. I was speaking to Dan Perry, my new bureau chief, who talked me through the situation, asking questions, some of which I couldn't answer. I grabbed a nearby man to get him to tell me what had happened but he only spoke Hebrew, so I handed him the phone to talk to Dan.

Elizabeth had got closer to the bus. She'd photographed the bomber's body parts: a foot lying on a footpath on the other side of the road from me and the man's torso, his face leaning on the cement with eyes closed. The bomber looked like he was sleeping, but he was missing the rest of his body. He'd been torn into pieces in the explosion, and the pieces had been flung everywhere. It transpired that he'd been trying to get on the bus but the driver refused him entry, so he detonated his package, blowing his body sky-high and blasting all the windows on board. His bits had landed up to 70 metres away from the explosion site.

It dawned on me how disturbingly close we had been to this bombing at the time it occurred. I stayed around while Elizabeth returned to the office to file her pictures. More and more journalists arrived. The police chiefs and mayor turned up and started doing interviews. The area was cordoned off, and we were pushed back further and further away from the scene. I watched as a truck came and towed the bus away, its back windows hanging from their hinges. This was the first time I'd been anywhere near a suicide bombing. But it wouldn't be the last.

When we finally finished work that day Elizabeth and I went to The Artists House and got very drunk. This was something neither of us had faced before. A Guadalajara native, Elizabeth had worked the length and breadth of Central and South America, covering every kind of natural disaster. She'd happened upon mounds of bodies washed up from floods and set on fire, the only way to dispose of them quickly before disease could spread to the survivors. Drug cartels, crime lords and earthquakes—she'd seen and photographed them all. But this was new. We sat there facing each other, trying to imagine what the man had been thinking to have consciously done this. *How depressed would you have to be to think that blowing yourself up was the only option you had?*

'He'd have gotten up this morning knowing it would be his last day,' Elizabeth said. Before Osama bin Laden used suicide attackers in his Holy War as a political/faith-driven act, Palestinians blamed despair and hopelessness for their situation as the biggest reason young men and women were drawn to become suicide bombers.

We rang our colleagues to talk to them. *How do you deal with this? You've seen worse; what was it like for you?* And we drank steadily. By the end of the night we were so far gone that we couldn't even remember who we'd called on the phone. We were so drunk that Dudu, the restaurant's owner, drove us home; we left Elizabeth's car behind. Elizabeth came up to my place because she was too drunk to fiddle with the ten differ-ent locks on her ground-floor flat and we both collapsed onto my bed.

At 8 a.m. the next morning the office rang. There'd been another suicide bombing at Kfar Saba. This time, two teens were killed along with the suicide bomber. It was my day off and I was meant to pack — I had an early flight home the next day. *Could I go?*

'Okay,' I said into the phone, then looking up at Elizabeth I asked: 'Where is Kfar Saba?'

Elizabeth and I left my apartment and took a cab back to The Artists House so I could collect my bag and she could get her car. We initially had trouble communicating with the taxi driver — he spoke bad French but no English; we spoke even worse French but no Hebrew. Somehow we managed to talk in French and I told him where I was going. I asked him if he would be my driver for the day. He agreed so we dropped Elizabeth off at her car and then headed for Kfar Saba, over an hour's drive north from Jerusalem.

I sat huddled in the back, my sunglasses firmly in place to hide my sunken eyes. Avi, the driver, stopped at a grocery store on the way and came out with cigarettes for himself and a large bottle of water for me. I hugged it to myself throughout the drive while I rang some of the people I'd called the previous night, apologising for disturbing them with my drunken ramblings. They were very understanding.

On our drive Avi told me he was a former Golani soldier, of the feared Golani Brigade. It was one of the toughest divisions in the Israeli army. He was nearly seven-foot tall and built like a brick wall. He was a great guide for me that day because no one was able to stand up to him or refuse his questions and overtures. Whenever we stopped to ask directions or came close to being turned away from travelling down certain roads the police had blocked off due to security fears, he would say something or get out of the car and talk to whoever was involved. Magically, the problem was solved.

The bombing had happened at a petrol station and, considering its proximity to the fuel, it was a wonder everything hadn't gone up in flames. When we arrived the body of the bomber was already wrapped in a black plastic bag and tagged; the two teenage schoolboys, who'd lost their lives as well, had already been taken away. The area was cordoned off and we weren't allowed to approach. Avi went up to the police to find out what was going on. I watched as some ultra-Orthodox men wearing fluorescent vests cleared the site. I learnt later that they were volunteers who responded to all the suicide bombings to collect every bit of flesh. It was a grisly task, but a necessary one to ensure a proper Jewish burial.

We weren't getting much information at the site, so we decided to go to the hospital to talk to the injured. The police at the site said four people were hurt. I followed Avi as he strode through the corridors of the Kfar Saba hospital towards the children's ward. In my stupor I marvelled at him, hunching over and quietly whispering in a man's ear, asking a doctor where an injured teenager was. He was a gentle giant.

We circled the main desk and came to a door and walked inside. There lay Rafael Somer, fifteen years old, with his arm strapped and cuts still fresh on his cherubic face. His father and mother were standing by him, his sister behind them. His brother sat leaning against the wall, the two back legs of the chair supporting him as he swung back, head tilted towards the ceiling. I quietly asked if it was alright for me to question Rafael. Avi repeated the question in Hebrew to the family. But it was Rafael's sister who agreed to talk with me.

She told me Rafael had been standing with his friends when they saw a man in a black leather jacket walk up to them. They were seminary students and it struck them as odd that a secular-looking man, perhaps an Arab, wanted to talk to them at all. Secondly, he was wearing a black leather jacket in stifling heat. Rafael was used to seeing only ultra-Orthodox Jews wear so much clothing in hot weather. It alarmed him so he took a couple of steps away from his friends as they talked to the man. Those few steps saved his life. Only moments later, the man detonated the explosives he had hidden under his jacket.

Rafael was lucky to emerge with just those cuts. Many bombers had begun to use ball bearings, rusty nails or any kind of metal they could get their hands on. Quite a number of those who didn't die at the hands of the bombers were maimed or lacerated for life — blinded or paralysed or comatose; their bodies were full of shrapnel that would never be removed because it was too dangerous to try.

Rafael's parents were almost mute throughout my conversation with their daughter. They seemed to be in shock. I wondered, *How do you continue to allow your son to catch a bus to school? How much of your life would you have to change to avoid scenarios that seemed humdrum and banal before, but full of peril now?*

It only got worse when I returned from my break in Sydney. The number of dead began to rise and the Israelis reacted by bombing Palestinian police installations and firing rockets at militants and their alleged workshops. Things deteriorated even more in 2001, when a suicide bomber attacked a discotheque in Tel Aviv and killed more than 20 young nightclubbers.

The day of that bombing, 1 June 2001, I'd just finished a long stint of work covering the funeral of Faisal al-Husseini, the PLO's representative to Jerusalem. He was so respected across the region that the Israeli government allowed Palestinians from the West Bank to come to Jerusalem to mark his funeral. It was quite a spectacle to see bands of Palestinians walking, driving and chanting as they entered Jerusalem, a city denied to them for so long. The day had passed without incident, seemingly matching the Israeli gesture of goodwill, but then I heard about the bombing while I was sitting in the garden restaurant of the American Colony.

I rang the office to see if I should go to Tel Aviv to cover the story. Jerome Delay was with me and waited to see what I would do. Dan at first told me to head to the office, so we jumped in the car and headed in that direction. Then Dan rang and said he'd changed his mind: 'Go to Tel Aviv.' Jerome hit the brakes so hard they screeched as he did a U-turn. But he was heading towards his apartment, not Tel Aviv.

'We're taking the bike,' he said.

Shit. I looked at my outfit. I was wearing three-quarter length pants, heels and a skimpy top—we had been planning to go clubbing after dinner. I wasn't exactly dressed for a bike ride. Jerome gave me one of his sweaters, which covered most of my body, and I climbed onto the back of his bike, hooking my stiletto heels onto the small pedals.

My helmet didn't have a protective visor.

'Just close your eyes and hold on tight,' Jerome said. I did. We got there in 20 minutes—a trip that normally took about 50. We'd gone some 200 kilometres per hour, he said.

When we got to the area, Jerome ran off to negotiate his way past the police cordons. I looked up at the Dolphinarium nightclub and tried to describe the scene to Yoav Appel, a new reporter who would soon become my flatmate, on the other end of the phone at the office. I needed to find a witness but barely anyone there spoke English. I began grabbing people and shoving the phone in their hands so that Yoav could speak to them in Hebrew and get their details. There was one guy wearing a pink shirt with a white singlet underneath.

'This guy's got blood on him,' I said to Yoav before passing over the phone. I felt a moment of shame as I watched him talk in sobs to Yoav.

What's going on with me? What have I become? I was looking for bloodied and traumatised people. I hated myself for charging at these distressed people, crying and confused as they staggered away from the bombed-out club. Each time someone walked towards me, I took a deep breath before going up to them, touching their arm lightly and saying, 'Excuse me' in Hebrew before handing them the phone. For many of them it was just a reflex action: take the phone and talk to the voice. It was also probably therapeutic for them to get it out and tell someone what they'd just seen, but it made me feel awful.

This was one of those moments when I hated my job. The last thing I would have wanted was someone shoving a microphone or tape recorder in my face and asking me how it felt to escape death while others were blown to bits in front of me. Yet that was what I had to do. I often feel that journalists spend their time being either vultures or dogs. We pick at something that's bleeding and tear it to pieces or we sit there waiting, content with whatever scraps get thrown our way.

From that moment a cycle of violence and counter-violence followed. The Israelis would kill a militant. That militant's group would vow revenge, setting off another suicide bombing. The Israelis would then use F16 jets against the Palestinians in Gaza, setting off even more violent retaliations. I grew tired of hearing the rounds of official condemnation coming from the Palestinian Authority after each suicide bombing. Words just meant nothing. If they knew who was behind the attacks, why weren't they stopping them? It is not easy to keep a secret in the Palestinian areas. If you wanted to speak to a militant, you could ask someone who would speak to someone else and eventually you would get the person you were after. All it required was *wasta*, Arabic for 'connections', 'influence', 'clout'—knowing some-one who could get you what you needed.

On one occasion two friends of mine were 'kidnapped' by Palestinian militants in Gaza. Word about it came to us through sources in Ramallah but as soon as we told our reporters in Gaza and they told the security officials there, my friends were released almost immediately. Mohammed Dahlan, the Palestinian security chief, even took them to dinner to apologise. Despite journalists being shot in the course of covering clashes, we never really feared for our lives in this way. Journalists, with their column space and air time, were largely welcomed by all sides.

Whenever there was a bombing I would get a call, asking me to go to Gaza to await the inevitable Israeli retaliation.

Palestinians would be rushing to the shops to buy bread and milk and anything else they needed in case they couldn't leave their homes for a long period of time. I would often get the call from the office for me to go to Gaza while I was still at the scene of the latest suicide bombing. Once in Gaza I'd look anxiously up at the sky for helicopters as Najib Abu Jobein, the APTN cameraman, sped through the sandy alleyways of the small neighbourhoods, driving from one office to another, talking on the phone to the different body-guards to let them know we were on our way.

I'd be terrified as Najib and I raced to the different militant leaders' homes or offices to get their reaction to the bombings. I would pray that, if the Israelis were going to retaliate, do it after we've gone. I had no problem getting Abdel Aziz al-Rantisi's final quote, just as long as I was out of the Hamas leader's building first.

At al-Rantisi's home we would climb the stairs and sit in his stifling sitting room while he asked all about the bombing that had just taken place: How many were killed? How had it happened? I can't say for sure that he showed grim satisfaction that the attacks had taken place. He never expressed surprise at the bombings. The Palestinians were expected to act in any way they could to take on Israel, he would say. He never let on whether he was involved or knew it would happen beforehand—just that there would be more of the same while the situation continued as is. As we scampered out to escape any coming Israeli retaliation I would always wonder, *How much do you really know? Is this all just an act, for us?*

The bombings altered my habits. When I was in Jerusalem I never took the bus. I resisted walking down Jaffa Road and kept away from crowds. I watched everyone who entered The Artists House as we sat there eating and drinking, wondering if the bag on their shoulders contained a bomb. Loud noises would startle me. Other people also became irritable with each other, their patience worn to its limits. Fights would start over parking spaces, tables at restaurants, talking during a movie at the cinema. I was at the mall one day, standing in line for the fitting room at Zara, one of my favourite boutique stores. I was at the head of the queue when a girl strode past the line and stood next to me. I looked at her and then turned to look at the girls waiting behind me.

'Um, you know, there's a line there. People have been waiting,' I said. She didn't even blink.

'If you don't like it, go back to the country you came from,' she snapped at me. I rolled my eyes and made sure I went ahead of her anyway. I was feeling rather combative myself and I would have argued with her if she had decided to push in, but she didn't. The lack of patience everyone else seemed to exhibit had rubbed off on me too.

For the first time in my short journalistic career, I also got to see what the other side of life was for a war correspondent. I watched as colleagues went home with colleagues for the night, and forgot all about it the next day. I watched as grown women argued over visiting male photographers and journalists and who would sleep with whom. I watched as married or attached people threw the rule book out the window and lived 'for the moment' in the arms of a willing partner for one night only. Not everyone, of course, lived like this, but many did. It was transcendence they sought, a temporary softness in the middle of all the hardness that surrounded us.

It affected us all in different ways. Charging uninvited into closed-off areas, we were accused everyday of showing bias by all and sundry, no matter what side they were on. We were the foreign press. We worked hard, played hard, got drunk, stayed up till the early hours, then rose early, ready for the next day's action. We were immune to the blood, the dead, the crying; joked about how we just missed getting shot; were cynical of new peace endeavours. We were always streaking ahead to the front, to be first with the story. You were known by how many prizes you'd won and how many conflicts you'd covered. I was a novice, but this scene among war journalists was being played out all over the world and always would be; Sarajevo, Sierra Leone, Dili, Baghdad, Jerusalem and more war zones yet to come.

For me, for months after I split with my ex-boyfriend, this way of being seemed to make sense. I didn't believe there was such a thing as a committed man, and here around me was the proof I needed. This was unfair perhaps, but I was in an unforgiving frame of mind. The whole code of behaviour left me cold. Men were random, faceless figures. Personality didn't really matter. Emotions weren't allowed. You couldn't need someone, or project the idea of a future when you lived like this. In a world of temporary, you couldn't cling to something and make it permanent. It didn't work like that here.

One of my friends told me that, when she first met me, while I was going through this phase, I was, 'all sharp edges, you didn't let anyone get close to you, you had a fuck-them-all attitude. Only months later, when you felt you could, did you let us see the warm and loving Jamie hidden underneath.' It also didn't help that the worsening political situation around us only intensified our emotions and made the whole concept of living for now and forgetting about tomorrow much more palatable. After all, we could die tomorrow while covering the clashes.

Was it easier to deal with a guilty conscience this way, especially when assuaged with alcohol? Perhaps. While I had my
occasional share of fun, I never made it my mission to get
lucky and pull someone for the night as many others did. I
always derived more enjoyment from drinking myself silly
and being one of the last holding up the bar, dancing and
fending off ridiculous chat-up lines from forward Israeli men.
Once, as I was sitting at a bar drinking, a tall Israeli came
up to me, held my face in his hands and asked, 'What do I
have to do to become your husband?'

'Well,' I said, 'you can let go of my face for a start.'

The audacity of some Israeli males always surprised me.
They didn't cloak their intentions when it came to chatting up
women. And the women were equally forward. I thought this
was almost symptomatic of Israeli society. It looked to me like
a pattern had been set.

The young men and women would meet during army
service, many of them only 21 at the time, get married and
swiftly have children. Fresh out of university, the intensity
of their life-or-death army vocation brought out heightened
emotions in the new conscripts. Later many would divorce
and their children would grow up travelling back and forth
between each parent and their grandparents. There were so
many men and women in their early thirties who were single
with children.

I dated an Israeli guy for a very brief period, for reasons I
could never explain to anyone. He was incredibly abrasive,
but the more obnoxious he was, the more I was attracted
to him. He was the loud, right-wing Israeli and I was the
pacifist, liberal Westerner. It was bizarre and perverse, the
way we behaved together, when we couldn't get past our
mutual dislike of each other's personalities. I cooked him
dinner one night and at the end of the meal he told me that

he'd once been the chef at a top Jerusalem restaurant. I'd wanted the meal to be perfect and I wanted to impress him and all the time he'd been duping me just to rile me, and I was riled. He'd do anything to annoy me and I quickly realised I wanted to do the same. He had very strong opinions on everything—political positions that I disagreed wildly with. One night I met him at The Artists House wearing a large silver cross around my neck. I didn't wear it out of any particular religious motivation, but the sight of it threw him completely off guard.

'I had no idea you were so religious,' he said, before pausing a moment then asking whether I'd consider converting to Judaism because 'it was the best religion'. I told him I was perfectly happy with the religion I already had. Setting each other off was our version of fun. We drifted apart because the worse the intifada got the less we had to talk about to each other. He couldn't understand why I would willingly cover stories in the Palestinian areas and I couldn't understand why he wouldn't reason with me. He didn't want to debate issues, he didn't even want to try. He refused to entertain any sympathy for the Palestinians, even as I tried desperately to maintain a balance in my views. I saw more of the Palestinians than he did and was more critical and upset over their situation because of that, but in my own way, I could understand both sides. That didn't mean I agreed with anyone in particular; I just grew more and more cynical the worse things got.

CHAPTER FOURTEEN

One hot August night in Baghdad, Iraq, during the summer of 2003, I watched al-Jazeera television report on the killing of Ismail Abu Shanab, one of Hamas' top leaders in the Gaza Strip. My first thought turned to Hiba, his youngest daughter, who would have been about four years old when her father was killed in the Israeli rocket attack. I remembered meeting her years earlier at Abu Shanab's house in the Jabaliya refugee camp. Elizabeth, Aiman and I were sitting in the living room waiting for him to appear when she came in, staring at us with enormous green eyes, looking annoyed.

I remembered the living room, the walls adorned with maps of pre-1948 Palestine, framed Islamic verses and in one corner a computer and a bookcase choked with books. After Abu Shanab came in, it took about fifteen minutes before he was able to look me in the eye when he answered my questions. I couldn't make out whether it was because I was a woman or a journalist. He also seemed embarrassed every time the little girl charged into the room, having a sip of his glass of Coke, standing in front of me and staring. I laughed and tried to say hello to her, but she ignored me. Her name meant 'Gift' in Arabic, a gift, Abu Shanab said, because she was born after he emerged from eight years in Israeli prisons.

Standing in my tenth floor suite in al-Hamra Hotel in August 2003, watching the angry crowd on TV trying to pull the bodies out of the smouldering car that Abu Shanab and his bodyguard had been travelling in, I thought of the confluence of radical talk and behaviour, and the impressionable young minds of children. I thought of how the images routinely displayed on Arab television affected the mindset of those most likely to be in front of the screens: kids. A fellow journalist once said she thought Palestinian children had the eyes of 50-year-old people, because they'd already seen and heard so much. Propagandists also played up the alarming number of children who'd been killed in the conflict, to draw in younger minds to their cause.

That was one of the things that bothered me most, the way children were planted right at the forefront of this never-ending conflict. They saw everything, heard everything; they were used to the sounds of shooting, rocket attacks, soldiers at checkpoints and military tanks. Their minds were shaped by the time they went to high school and everything they heard there only cemented what they already believed. *It was everywhere I went. If I couldn't escape it, how could little children?*

I was once in Nablus in August 2001 with AP stringer Mohammed Daraghmeh. We were doing a story on Palestinian collaborators and on how local vigilantes were killing them in the street because they felt Palestinian justice was too slow to act. Even if collaborators were condemned to death legally, none had been executed since those first executions in January 2001—Arafat was still smarting from the international condemnation heaped on him for allowing those to take place. My friend Matthew McAllester from *Newsday*, a Long Island newspaper, had suggested I speak to Hossam Khader, a local Fatah leader in Balata refugee camp.

The camp was on the outskirts of town where many of the gunmen lived. It was at their hands and others living in different refugee camps around the West Bank and Gaza that local justice was dished out. Khader was one of the most vocal proponents of punishing collaborators as an example to anyone who contemplated informing for money. The rewards by Israelis to Palestinians who provided information on militants and their movements were great — virtually a livelihood, because they often received ID cards that allowed them to travel further than their neighbours, and to live in better conditions.

We went upstairs to Khader's office where he was waiting for us. He was in his late 30s or early 40s and was cross-eyed, a condition I later learnt was a consequence of beatings he endured in an Israeli jail. Matthew had told me that Khader had said something about Arafat being displeased with him because Khader wanted to change the Palestinian Authority's structure. He wanted greater transparency and to get rid of the corruption plaguing the administration. He pointed fingers and named names, and Arafat wanted him silenced. At one point in our interview, Khader very proudly showed me a fax someone from the Palestinian Authority had sent him. Scribbled at the top he claimed was Arafat's writing. It called for Khader to be 'spoken to'. He was giddy as he talked of how much of a thorn in Arafat's side he was and he giggled as he spoke.

Khader enjoyed being interviewed so much he invited us back to his house afterwards. We climbed several flights of stairs and walked into his lushly carpeted living room, complete with chintzy furniture and mirrored crystal cabinets. We sat while his two children raced around the room. The boy and girl both had eyes of an amazing colour — a dirty sea-green. Mohammed told me Khader had divorced but kept the children. I sank into an overstuffed couch and accepted the coffee his little girl brought us. She was very shy and rushed back into the kitchen when I thanked her.

Two men walked into the room, AK-47s slung over their shoulders. One was skinny with dark black curly hair. The other was tall and stocky with a buzz cut.

When we stood up to greet them Mohammed exclaimed: 'This man is the most wanted man by Israel!' and shook the stocky man's hand. I stepped back a little and hesitated as he thrust his hand out to me, but I took it as I looked at this man with bulging eyes.

'I'm Jamie,' I said to him.

'Maslama,' he murmured in reply. I looked at Mohammed, hoping he would elaborate.

'Maslama is the nephew of Thabet Thabet,' Mohammed said. I continued looking at him. It still didn't mean anything to me.

'He's accused of murdering the two Israelis in Tulkarem in January.'

I looked again at Maslama. I had been in Taba when the Israeli delegation hurried back to Jerusalem, halting the talks, after the two Tel Aviv restaurateurs were gunned down. Here in front of me was the man who'd done it. I'd never come face to face with a murderer who was happy to confess to the killing. We sat down and Khader's little girl came out again with red jelly for everyone to eat. His young son picked up one of the rifles and started running around the room with it. My attention was swinging between the silent killer in front of me and the young boy scampering wildly around the living room with a loaded automatic weapon.

'It's okay, I've got the safety lock on it,' the other guy, Majid al Masri, said after noticing my concern. I wanted to say something about the dangers of children with guns but, considering the present company, I held my tongue. I turned my focus onto Thabet while trying to give off an air of indifference—*How does one behave around a guy who's supposedly killed two people, especially when there is a loaded weapon by his feet?*

'Do you want to tell me what happened?' I asked him quietly, nudging Mohammed to press Maslama Thabet to speak. He didn't need much prompting.

Between spoonfuls of jelly, he spoke of how, after his uncle Thabet Thabet was shot and killed as he left his home on 31 December 2000, Maslama had plunged into a world of hurt. He was very close to his uncle—Greg Myre in our office had told me that Maslama Thabet had apparently spent most nights after his uncle's killing crying by Thabet Thabet's grave. One January day, Maslama's friends came to him and told him that two Israelis had come to Tulkarem and were having a meal at one of the restaurants. They charged into the restaurant wearing masks and grabbed the two men. Then, at point-blank range, Thabet lifted his pistol and shot them.

'For the first time I was able to sleep with my mind at peace,' he said quietly.

I concentrated on writing everything down, not letting the weight of his words affect me. Then I noticed that both the children were sitting down and listening. *They shouldn't be hearing this*, I thought. *It's not exactly a bedtime story.*

At this point al Masri interrupted.

'We wanted peace with Israel,' he said. 'Before this intifada, we were dealing with them normally.'

I'd also heard from Greg that before his uncle's death Maslama Thabet had kept his distance from the uprising. He had participated in a co-existence movement with Israelis his age and had advocated open dialogue between the two people. He came from an educated family and didn't take part in the violence, unlike many others who saw no other outlet or had a different analysis. But the death of his uncle changed all that. Maslama Thabet turned from being a quiet observer of the unfolding violence to one of its biggest supporters.

I looked over at Khader's son and thought about what his everyday life must have been like, sitting at home and watching gunmen parade through, playing with their guns as they spoke about killing Israelis. He didn't even have to turn on the television to know what was happening. He was living it here, in his loungeroom.

I was always overly affected whenever I saw children wrapped up in a conflict that they would only ever understand from one side. Death and anger claimed them and overruled the childhood they should have been having. To me, it didn't matter which side you were on, no matter what was said or how things were made to look, and no matter who thought who was dictating life to whom, innocent children were being caught up in the middle of a conflict they didn't have the maturity to understand.

In early 2001, our bureau set a project about a day in the life of the Palestinians and the Israelis. The day we covered the Israeli side, I was sent to an army reservist site. I interviewed men as old as 40, who were called up for military duty. These men had families and lives outside the army. The day we wrote about the Palestinians, Elizabeth and I went to Hebron. We were supposed to talk to a family confined to their house because of the stringent military curfew in the area. We walked the empty streets of central Hebron trying to find people to talk to. Anyone. We looked up at windows to see if anyone was peeking outside. No one.

We met up with Hazim, the local APTN cameraman, and as we turned into a small alleyway we heard a whimpering voice. We moved towards the sound until we spotted a young Palestinian girl who'd squeezed herself into the gateway of an Arab house so she couldn't be seen unless you walked right up to the entrance. She was crying and seemed extremely frightened. For a moment I was too scared to approach her — I thought she might have been rigged with explosives, which wasn't such a far-fetched thought — female suicide bombers were beginning to wreak havoc along with men.

'What's the matter?' Hazim asked her.

'I can't go home,' she said, sobbing.

'Where do you live?' I asked.

'In the Old City,' she said. I looked over at Hazim. He pointed in the direction of where we had come from. It was curfew and she was not supposed to be on the street.

'Why don't you go home?' I asked.

'Because the soldiers will hit me,' she said, and started crying again.

I told Elizabeth what was going on.

'Come with us. No one will hurt you if you come with us,' I said. I put out my hand to her to come. She could barely focus on putting one foot in front of the other; she was shaking and crying. Elizabeth and I looked at each other.

We turned the corner and came across two Israeli border policemen standing at a small checkpoint. They immediately asked for our ID cards and wanted to know why the girl was with us. We told them we were taking her home. They waved us through but one of the them deliberately dropped Hazim's press card on the ground. The policeman pretended he hadn't dropped it, that it was an accident, and told Hazim to pick it up. Hazim refused. He just stood there and waited for the policeman to stoop over and pick up the card, to return it to him just as he had handed it over to the policeman in the first place. We nervously waited until he did so.

We walked from the checkpoint into a small alley and came across three young Israeli women, their heads covered in scarves, one of whom was pushing a stroller. At this point the girl became very frightened, too scared to take another step. She wouldn't move. I told her to walk on my right side, alongside the wall, with me on the outside of her, protecting her from the women. Elizabeth later told me she'd seen one of the women bend down and pick up a rock, intending to throw it at the Palestinian girl who was with us.

A couple of border police guards were nearby and they approached us when they heard the women talking in Hebrew, directing their words at the Palestinian girl. All I knew was that the women sounded angry. The woman pushing the stroller had come towards us and aimed the stroller—with the baby inside—at the girl's feet, to trip her or hit her. I wasn't really sure what she was trying to do but I put my left foot out and the stroller hit my ankle instead. That's when the border police decided to intervene.

Placing a hand on the stroller, he told the woman to back away and she started yelling at him. I looked at the policeman gratefully, and told him we were just helping this girl get home, for obvious reasons. He walked with us as we turned into another, smaller alleyway and from there the young Palestinian girl said she was close to her home.

'Hurry up, go!' we said to her, and we watched as she slowly shuffled away at first, before breaking into a run and disappearing down the road. I wondered how long it would have taken her to get home if we hadn't seen her. Then the border policeman walked with us back past the Israeli women, in case they gave us trouble for helping the girl.

I often wondered how that Palestinian girl would have remembered that moment in her life. Would it have been any different from any other day in her twelve or so years? She'd have gone home and, if anyone had listened, she would have told them what happened and they would have probably cursed Israelis yet again. Would she ever consider getting along with and living peacefully near those she had only heard bad things about? Or near those who only confirm those bad things as true when she comes face to face with them?

For most young Israelis the only contact they have with Palestinians is at checkpoints. This sets up an atmosphere of distrust to begin with, because every person heading towards them might be a suicide bomber. After four years of violence, rocket attacks and bombings there was nary a person on either side who hadn't been affected by the conflict. Almost everyone would have lost someone to the violence, or been injured, or was related to someone who had experienced it. It was hardly an environment that encouraged compromise.

While I immersed myself in this story and this life and this land, I lost day-to-day, intimate contact with my family. By March 2002, I hadn't been home in over a year, which greatly distressed my tight-knit family. I felt guilty about missing special moments—my mother's 50th and my father's 60th, in particular—because I knew they would not be able to move beyond my absence to enjoy themselves properly. I was wanted at home. I would tell my parents, devout Catholics that they are, that I was going to different churches in Bethlehem, Nazareth and Jerusalem, and lighting candles for them on those special days. My father would momentarily forget lecturing me about staying safe to say how lucky I was to be there and to be able to pray at these holy places, where every Christian dreamt of going.

My sisters became more distant on the phone. There wasn't much more they could say beyond, 'Please, be careful', to which I would respond by quickly reassuring them that I was fine. Christine had just started a new job and Stefanie had finished high school. Maria was still working at her job, which I never understood and couldn't explain to anyone who asked. I felt guilty. I had no idea of what was really going on in their lives beyond these sorts of lonely facts. I also felt they couldn't possibly begin to understand what I was doing on a daily basis and I deliberately didn't talk too much about my working life because I didn't want them to worry more than they did already. There was a silent reproach in their voices. They thought my wild behaviour was driving my parents mad with anxiety and I was too absorbed in my own adventures to take responsibility for the consequences of my actions.

It was too hard to explain to them that this was my life now; this is what it had become. Was it making me *happy?* There never seemed any point in asking myself something like that. How could covering death and destruction and living with the daily threat of it bring anyone happiness? But I had to feel like I was achieving something, that I was doing something to make all of this—the heartache, the anxiety, the stress—somehow worthwhile. I was running out of answers.

CHAPTER FIFTEEN

When I returned to Jerusalem for Arafat's funeral in 2004, my friends and I agreed that the incursion into Jenin in March 2002 had provided the climax to the epic struggle we had been engrossed in for so long. Jenin changed us all. At the time it happened, Arafat was holed up in Ramallah and there was practically a suicide bombing every day. The rhetoric sprouted from both sides of the political divide had grown ever stronger and no one was safe.

On 27 March 2002, our Jewish staffers had left the office to go home and observe Passover. Only Karin and I were in the office. Since I couldn't understand Hebrew, my job involved answering phones and swapping the tapes to record the news and play it back for Karin when she needed to hear bulletins again. At about 8 p.m., a radio news flash reported that there'd been a suicide bombing at a hotel in Netanya, on Israel's northern coast.

'Ring Jason—ask if he can go,' Karin said. I had to make the phone call to him that every reporter dreaded hearing, 'Can you go and cover this suicide bombing?' For us it meant going out, invariably in the dark, and trying to find a cab that would take you all the way to where you needed to go—usually at an exorbitant rate. There you would remain as long as necessary, filing quotes, colour and detail from the scene back to the office. If you were lucky, sometimes you could hitch a ride to the scene with photographers, who had their own cars to cart all their equipment. Most often, though, you were left to your own devices regarding transportation, and it was the amount of shekels you had in your pockets at the time that would finance the trip.

Karin filed news bulletins with every update of the death toll. I rang the police and ambulance to get official numbers and also contacted the stringers to see if they had gathered reactions from any of the militant groups. The death toll kept growing and growing. This was a big one.

The bomber had walked into the dining room of the Park Hotel as 250 guests, families celebrating Passover, were sitting down for the meal. It was one of the holiest days on the Jewish calendar. The television reports started showing footage of blood sprayed on the ceiling of the dining room; upturned strollers in the room and white tablecloths dripping red with blood. All the threats Sharon had made about hitting back at the Palestinians seemed ominous.

Two days later I was asleep when I got a call from the office telling me to come in and work. It was Good Friday and I had really wanted to go to church, even if just briefly. I never usually had the time to go to mass but on this, the holiest day in the Christian calendar, I really wanted to make the effort.

'It's Good Friday,' I mumbled into the phone.

'Well there are tanks in Arafat's compound. They're asking you to come in,' said Mark, the night editor who was wrapping up his shift. Annoyed, I got dressed and went in.

Most of the people in our office had gone home early, as they'd normally do on a Friday as the Sabbath got underway. It pissed me off that I had to come in and work — *Is my Christian holiday less important?* But it was also still *Pesagot* — Passover. What was supposed to have been a quiet time in the office became the busiest since the uprising began in September 2000 . Everyone abandoned their time off and came in to work. We sent out for large orders of food from east Jerusalem for the whole office, since everything in west Jerusalem was shut down for Passover.

Arafat's offices were surrounded. Ramallah was under siege. And just like in September 2000, news organisations brought in more journalists to help out. Israel called the action 'Operation Defensive Shield'. Whole army units moved into Ramallah and blocked all the exits. Ordinary Palestinians bolted themselves inside their houses while militias engaged in running street battles with the soldiers. An Italian photographer who'd been trailing a group of militiamen was shot and killed. Hundreds of Palestinian men were rounded up, put onto trucks and taken in for questioning. The UN Security Council passed a resolution calling on Israel to withdraw its troops. But Israel wouldn't listen. Instead, Sharon sent tanks into Beit Jalla and Bethlehem as well. The shooting in Bethlehem sent gunmen scurrying into the Church of the Nativity, where they took refuge with priests and nuns. Little did they know that they would remain there for 38 days and would only finally leave after their exile to Gaza and several European countries had been negotiated between clerics and Palestinian and Israeli officials.

We cracked joke after joke when we first heard about the gunmen in the church.

'It's probably the first time any of them have been near a church. Maybe they went in for confession.' Anything to lighten the mood. It was rather ironic that these hardened fighters suddenly had to come face to face with old nuns and priests. The prospect of conversions or sudden illuminations seemed humorously plausible.

Churches were closed and there was little celebration that Easter. How could I explain any of this to my parents when they called? As it turned out they already knew because they, like the rest of the world, were watching it on television. This was a notch up from the standard violence and chaos that had plagued this place for the past two years. The war in Afghanistan was ebbing and the world's attention reverted to this latest unholy battle in this holiest of places, where the Israelis and the Palestinians were still skirmishing.

Sharon wanted to expel Arafat. The Israeli Cabinet had met regularly to decide what to do about him but the pressure from the international community was clear: do nothing except ease the siege. While Sharon refused to lift the blockade, he couldn't move against the Palestinian leader either. At one point he called Arafat an 'enemy' and said he was no longer a partner for peace. He declared Arafat would be isolated politically, as well as physically. How much difference this would actually make wasn't clear. Arafat had been restricted to Ramallah for months now. I couldn't help wondering how much more action Sharon could really take.

It was becoming harder and harder to get information from the towns that were cordoned off. We called the hospitals routinely for updates. They reported there were bodies of gunmen in the streets but no one could reach them, so the number of actual dead was never accurate. Then the army declared all of Ramallah a closed military zone. The idea that

an entire town could be shut off to journalists was preposterous to us so many of the foreign press ignored the
edict. Then soldiers shot over the heads of journalists to
warn them away. We carried on as best we could in a worsening situation.

The army denied it was detaining hundreds of Palestinian
men, even though several journalists had witnessed their
seizure. Power and water were cut off in many areas. Telephone lines were down. Shops were closed. People were
running out of supplies. The situation was becoming desperate. The soldiers took over entire buildings, staking out
rooftop positions, sandbagging windows and digging
trenches. They made it clear they were there for the long haul.

It didn't end in Ramallah, Beit Jalla and Bethlehem. Soon
Nablus and nearby Jenin were under Israeli control. And
soon, murmurs began about mass killings in the Jenin
refugee camp.

Where did the rumour about Jenin start? It wasn't clear
to us. We listened as whispers of wrongdoing rose into cries
of massacre. We heard stories of mass killings, of bodies
being taken away in secret, under the cover of darkness. The
whispers grew louder and louder, the rumours appeared to be
turning into fact. But we needed to find out what was going
on in the refugee camp ourselves.

Jerome Delay, who had flown in from Paris to help out
with the coverage, made his way to Jenin with Greg Myre.
They went in one of AP's bulletproof Jeeps. Getting into the
camp was nigh on impossible. All the roads were blocked—it
was still declared a closed military zone. Even people inside
Jenin couldn't have known what was going on because they
weren't allowed to leave their homes. People we tried calling
in the area could only repeat the speculation they'd heard
from others in the camp.

By this time Israel had taken over six Palestinian towns in the West Bank: Ramallah, Qalqiliya, Tulkarem, Nablus, Bethlehem and Jenin. The fiercest fighting raged in Jenin and Nablus. Before the army moved in, militants in these towns had bragged about plans to rig the main streets with explosives and booby-traps to welcome the Israelis. They planned to put up a fight and they were surprisingly organised, especially in Jenin. They had even ambushed Israeli soldiers on one day, killing thirteen. About 23 soldiers died altogether from the actions in that camp. The gunmen of Jenin refugee camp became heroes in the rest of the West Bank and Gaza. People in Gaza began naming their newborns 'Jenin' after the town and its battles.

As the situation and story accelerated, planeloads of foreign press arrived to provide coverage, just as they had when the intifada broke out in September 2000. Some 1600 Palestinians were detained by Israeli soldiers; pictures of men blindfolded, with numbers scrawled on their forearms, prompted an outcry within Jewish quarters as well as the international community. Arafat used these pictures to draw comparisons between the numbered prisoners and the Jews similarly treated when shipped off to concentration camps in Nazi Germany. It was a bad turn for the Israeli military which was already doing its best to shield its actions from the media.

I watched with interest as camera crews followed and taped soldiers looking for Marwan Barghouti in Ramallah. I wanted to see what Barghouti would do now, this man who insisted he would be strong. This was the moment he'd always talked about. But he'd gone into hiding. His wife, Fadwa, told reporters through a window in their apartment that she didn't know where he was. His son Qassam, the 'spoilt brat' I had met nearly two years ago, was detained and beaten before being released.

I was having dinner at The Artists House one night when my boss Dan called me and asked if I'd go to Jenin at first light to take over from Greg, who was now back in Jerusalem. For the first time in a long while, I was apprehensive about going into the field. I stopped by Greg's house to borrow his helmet and to get some insight into what he saw as the risks of being in Jenin. It was so dangerous now you couldn't take chances.

Fighting raged in a number of areas inside the camp and soldiers were trying to prevent anyone from entering. About 13 000 of the camp's residents had fled, emerging with stories of mass slaughter that no one could verify. Greg had been able to get inside the camp. He and Jerome were among the first journalists to get in, but they had not got far enough to see much of the destruction.

His advice to me: 'Try and get inside—right into the middle of the camp. That's where much of the destruction is supposed to have happened.'

I awoke the next morning, the sun not yet up, my little red suitcase packed and ready—I knew I'd be gone for a while. I meet Rawhi Rizam, the APTN cameraman, outside the office where we'd arranged for him to pick me up. It was still early, about 5 a.m. All I wanted to do was sleep. We had to drive along the roads leading to Nazareth because we were in a soft car—a civilian car. The roads in the West Bank were punctuated with checkpoints and roadblocks. We were to meet up with Jerome and go in with him because he had the bullet-proof car or, as we called it, the hard car.

The closer we got to our destination, the greater the pit in my stomach grew. I was feeling increasingly anxious but I tried to mask it by making idle talk with Rawhi. Neither of us knew what we were getting ourselves into. Two hours of driving later, we reached the Palestinian town of Salfit, just inside the border near the Israeli town of Afula. We met Jerome there with two other carloads of photographers and press, all trying to get into Jenin. This was where the story was now. Jenin was inaccessible and anything coming out of it would be news—perhaps even an exclusive.

About ten of us crammed into the hard car. Jerome began to drive but when we came to a junction we could see an Israeli army Jeep coming towards us from our left. A voice shouted something in Hebrew to us through a megaphone. We couldn't understand what he was saying, but I think he wanted us to stop. Jerome drove off in the other direction. I looked back and saw another Jeep had joined the first in the chase. *This is ridiculous*, I thought. *It's not like we could get away very fast in this car—we'd be lucky to get to 100 kilometres an hour.* We were worried the soldiers would open fire on us. They had done so to other reporters.

'Jerome, we should stop,' several people chorused. We pulled over. The soldiers had their guns pointed straight at us. We all climbed out with our hands up.

'We don't understand Hebrew,' I said as loud as I could. One of the soldiers walked up to Jerome and started telling him off for not listening to him when he told us to stop. Then we were all escorted to their base outside Salfit where they said they would check our credentials.

'Are we under arrest?' Jerome asked. He didn't get an answer.

The base looked like a permanent army camp with its rows of tanks and Jeeps and tents and sandbags and Israeli flags and outposts and roadblocks. *They are going to be here for a while*, I thought. We stood in the sun for hours, which we suspected was a deliberate move on their part to delay us. No one is supposed to move about after sunset—it's too dangerous and we would never risk it anyway. The longer we were detained at the base, the less time we would have to circumnavigate the roadblocks and get into the camp.

The Israelis were suffering significant negative public relations as a result of their current offensive. They were not disclosing many details of their operations or incursions inside Palestinian towns and were doing everything they could to block off towns at their entrances. They banned the press from entering—if you were busted, you were kicked out. Even the Red Cross and the United Nations couldn't get in.

Finally we were allowed to leave. It was now about 3 p.m. They'd let us go after verifying all our press cards and warning us not to try to get into Jenin again. We drove up to a hilltop and looked down at the Palestinian camp, which was barely visible to us from up there. I walked down the hill to a house and knocked on the door, asking if I could use the bathroom. The lady of the house ushered me in with a wave of her tea towel, pushing me towards the bathroom she said they didn't use—it was a Western bathroom with a proper toilet, as opposed to the Arab version with a hole in the floor. I smiled and said thank you, and when I emerged one of her daughters gave me a glass of water to drink. I accepted gratefully.

'Sit down, rest for a bit,' the mother said, perching on the edge of the sofa. 'You're trying to get into Jenin, aren't you?' I nodded, while drinking.

'Goodness only knows what has happened in there. We hear a lot of stories,' she said. She looked tired as she wiped her brow and smiled.

'Stay. Stay as long as you need to,' she offered before getting up and patting me on the shoulder.

'Thank you so much,' I said, handing her the glass, 'but I think they're waiting for me.'

'Well you be careful if you go there. There's army inside.' I nodded, said thank you again and waved as I walked out the door.

Normally I would have laughed off such concerns, but this time it really was different. Everyone was freaked. Journalists were being shot at with impunity. I really did have to be careful.

As we stood there waiting—I wasn't sure what for, but everyone just seemed to be waiting for something—some men approached us. It turned out they were from inside the camp and were among those who had been rounded up and detained. One man I spoke to said he had no idea what had happened to his family, whether they'd gone to a nearby village or stayed with relatives. He had no way of knowing. He couldn't contact them. He told me about his detention.

'We were all taken, one by one, into a room and questioned by an Israeli soldier who spoke Arabic. He knew who we all were. He was just checking up on each of us, and some of us he let go,' he told me. 'There was hardly enough food to go around or blankets to cover us while we slept.' He said his hands were tied the whole time.

'The whole time?' I asked him.

'Yes,' he said emphatically.

'Even when you went to the bathroom?' I asked. As banal a question as this sounds, it was one of those small details you never got any information on but always wondered about. At least, I always did. He nodded vigorously, showing me the marks on his wrists from the plastic binds.

'When I wanted to go to the bathroom the soldier undid my pants so I could piss.'

'Wow, really?' I blurted out, not knowing what else to say. It may not have been the most politically correct remark, but I was surprised that a soldier would do that. The man looked me in the eye and continued talking. He was completely unashamed about his experience, something I admired him for. He'd been detained for a week and then, he and some others were allowed to go. They were dropped off and told to make their own way home. They had been let go kilometres from anywhere during the night. They had still not got home; instead, they were living off the hospitality of the town we were near while they waited for Jenin to be free again so they could return there.

As I went to stand with the rest of the guys, one of the photographers said there'd been a suicide bombing in Jerusalem.

'Well, they won't be needing anything from us today,' Jerome said. The news coming out of the region would now be focused on the bombing, so the demand for something out of Jenin wouldn't be as great. The pressure was off us, at least for a little while. We could abandon our efforts for that day. Everyone turned away from the edge of the hill and left.

The AP people and most of the other press were staying at the Inter-Continental at the entrance to Nazareth, so Rawhi and I checked in there. We joined some of the others for dinner. While we ate our chicken Jim Nachtwey told us about going to the Oscars the month before because the film documentary about him, *War Photographer*, had been up for an award. Documentary makers had followed Jim around and had even attached a little camera to his own equipment to portray his work and his life. The film was due to debut at the Tel Aviv Film Festival in a few weeks' time and it was generating a lot of buzz. All we wanted to know, though, was what it was like to walk the red carpet with Hollywood stars. I wanted to know who he'd spotted. He told us how plain Julia Roberts was in the flesh, how normal and ordinary all the stars looked in reality.

'The only two who were absolutely beautiful in real life were Halle Berry and Uma Thurman,' Jim claimed.

What a world away it all seemed: the red carpet and the Academy Awards. And us sitting here in this roast chicken restaurant in Nazareth where we couldn't even get a drink.

The next morning we met in the hotel lobby at 5 a.m. Rawhi and I began what was to become for the next two weeks our daily routine for breakfast—some bread with cheese and as much coffee as we could swallow at that hour. It would be the only thing we'd eat the whole day, I was to discover.

There were four cars in the convoy that day, which was crazy. *How on earth are we supposed to operate?* It was so obvious, trawling around like a parade, that we were looking for a way into the camp. There was no way we were going to be able to sneak in anywhere. We drove for hours around villages, in little nooks of valleys, through fields of wheat and barley, just looking for an opening—a little road, a dirt track, anything that could lead us into Jenin and the camp. The camp was best reached through the town of Jenin, but there were neighbouring villages that could have also led us in. We had to try as many options as we could.

Hours later we'd made no progress. Eventually two of the other cars dropped off our little convoy, leaving just the ITN crew in their hard car and us. Our bulletproof car's windows were sealed shut so we couldn't hear anything from the outside and not much from the inside over the rattle of the car's engine. We got to one checkpoint and saw soldiers on the road but Jerome kept on driving, unaware that we'd been fired on for advancing. The ITN crew beeped Jerome on his walkie-talkie to tell him that the soldier had told us to stop. It was unnerving. We hadn't heard a thing. We turned around to try another way in.

We tried one of Jenin's main roads after hearing from other reporters that the road was clear of military presence. We came off a dirt track and cut into the main road, some distance from the actual entrance where soldiers manned a checkpoint. We drove by the charred rings of burnt tyres, mangled cars and steel beams littering the street, keeping an eye out for Israeli soldiers. Astonishingly, we found none and didn't stop until we reached the front of Jenin's Red Crescent Hospital. I went into the hospital while everyone else besieged a little store for drinks and ice cream. We were all sweating buckets in the heat.

As I walked inside I remembered my mission: 'Go and find the bodies. See if there really was a massacre.'

I didn't want to think about how morbid it was to be hunting for corpses. This was my job. In any case I wanted to know the truth myself. The army had reported about a hundred dead in Jenin, most of them gunmen. This couldn't be verified. The Palestinians claimed the dead were mostly civilians, so the rumour at least persisted on both sides. I knew that if I found out myself, I would know for sure.

Inside the hospital I asked the doctors whether they'd received any casualties.

'We haven't been able to get inside the camp for eight days, so we don't have any dead or injured, or anything,' one doctor told me. Their electricity supply had been cut and they existed on a generator. The lighting inside was dim.

'Is there anyone in the hospital who was inside that I can talk to?' I asked.

'There is a woman here who works as a nurse inside the camp. I'll find her,' the doctor said and walked away. I went outside to get a drink while I waited. Soon an old woman came out to talk to me. She sat beside me and I asked her what she'd seen, if it was true what people were saying.

'Oh, they're killing people everywhere, the soldiers that is. I saw them line men up with my own eyes. Against the wall they made them stand, then they fired on them and killed them all,' she said loudly. Her words attracted Palestinians standing nearby.

'You saw this?' I asked her.

'I swear. I saw it with my own eyes.' A teenage boy who had been listening then spoke up.

'I saw them myself, with my own two eyes,' he said, pointing to each of his eyes. 'I saw the machine tanks tread over bodies.'

'You did?' I asked. He nodded. 'When? When was this?' I asked him.

'A couple of days ago.'

'Where? Where did this happen?' I asked.

'Inside the camp, inside the camp,' he replied as he pointed towards the camp.

I sat back and regarded him. It was difficult for me to believe him. I had learnt that sometimes Palestinians could be their own greatest enemies. They were prone to exaggeration and I knew no matter how bad things ended up, they were never as bad as had been told to me. It was incredibly frustrating trying to figure out what was real and what wasn't, which was why we had to get in there ourselves to find out.

I caught up with the other journalists and found they'd all put on their flak jackets and helmets, ready to try to enter the camp. One of the photographers came up to me and said, 'Jim's wearing his flak jacket! Now I'm really scared!' It was meant as a joke, but it was probably one of the best indicators of how vulnerable we were feeling in this situation. Jim

Nachtwey rarely wore a flak jacket. He had covered riots and clashes and gun battles without a bulletproof vest, but this time he felt he needed it. It heightened my anxiety.

As we all walked down the hill on the outskirts of the town towards the camp we heard gunshots ring out. We stopped in our tracks. After a pause, we started walking again but more shots rang out.

'We're being warned,' said Tim, the ITN cameraman. So the thirteen or so of us decided to try a different approach. Wearing our 12-kilogram flak jackets and helmets and carrying the rest of our gear we snuck behind houses, ran across an open cemetery, scaled walls and ran up steep narrow alleyways, stopping every so often to catch our breath. This was one of those moments when I was thankful I wasn't a photographer or a cameraman. I had a small backpack with my notebook, phone, pen and bottled water. No camera lens, flash, spare battery or other equipment.

We stopped for a moment at the terrace of a Palestinian family's home even though I didn't want to stay long. They brought us glasses of water and opened their living room to us. We slumped on the couches, breathing heavily while we tried to think of where to go and what to do next. One of the boys of the family suddenly spoke up.

'You want to see bodies?' he asked. We said yes.

'I can show you,' he said. 'Follow me.'

We gingerly followed in the boy's footsteps through people's backyards. We threw ourselves onto the ground at one point when we heard the rumbling of a tank grow louder and louder until it felt like it was almost upon us. We just lay there silently, wishing it would move on. *What would they do if they found us?* I wondered. *What would happen to this family?* Another boy came up to us and told Rawhi that soldiers were going door-to-door asking, 'Where are the journalists?' They were looking for us. I didn't want to cause anyone any problems. We just wanted to get in and see some bodies before we were busted. Our mission was gruesome, but there it was.

We climbed over obstacles and ran as fast as we could until we reached the outskirts of the camp, where the cement-cubed apartments differed little from the town proper; it was just more cramped. The place was built on the hillsides, so the alleyways were steep. We ran up a 45-degree-angled path and rounded a building corner before I realised we'd crossed into the camp, although it still looked like Jenin to me. One of the first things we saw was an apartment that was still in pristine condition: the front doors were open but everything inside was untouched, even the glasses on the coffee table and the slippers by the door. The family who'd lived there had obviously left the doors open so soldiers wouldn't blow them up or break them down. The Israelis had presumably come in, searched the place, then left.

We climbed into a nearby building and found ourselves standing on a flat slab of concrete that I realised was someone's former living room. One wall had been taken out completely by a bulldozer so it was now like an outside terrace. The crystal cabinet, kitschy coffee table and chintz-covered sofas were covered in dust and cement. It looked like a doll house with the front wall removed and everything visible from the outside. Jerome went to open the locked front door of a neighbouring apartment but I screamed out to him: 'Don't! It could be booby-trapped!'

This was one of the things Greg had warned me about. Jenin gunmen had booby-trapped many of the doors to catch the Israeli soldiers by surprise, but the army was well aware of this tactic by now. They had begun using Palestinians as their own kind of human shields, forcing them to open doors.

Another method they used to avoid booby-traps was to enter homes through the side walls instead of their front doors, using sledgehammers to shatter the lightweight cinder blocks of which these places were constructed. They went from home to home smashing through the walls, thus avoiding any traps.

Finally the boy led us to a house and pointed up the stairs.

'Bodies,' he said, gesturing upwards.

The photographers scrambled up the stairs into the room, which was burnt black. The smell of burning still clung to the air, along with that of rotting flesh. I poked my head into the room to count the number of dead bodies. They were on top of each other in a charred mess; the smell was disgusting. Most of the photographers had covered their noses with scarfs or their shirts. I coughed, trying to get rid of the stench that was clogging up my nostrils and sticking to the roof of my mouth like bad peanut butter.

'Just breathe through your mouth,' Jim told me. 'You won't smell a thing.' I tried to concentrate on my job.

'How many can you see?'

'Three,' Jerome said.

'Any more?' I asked, before calling the office to report.

That was as far as we would go that day. It was getting late; we had to go back so the photographers could file their pictures. I couldn't find anyone to interview because there was no one around. I looked about me and saw deserted alleyways and shuttered windows. I couldn't even hear people talking as I had when I'd gone into Hebron. Clearly I wasn't going to get anyone to talk to me here. Plus, we were worried the soldiers would find us.

We ran back the way we'd come, climbing over walls, scraping knees and elbows, running through a cemetery, zigzagging between tombstones. All the time we had eyes and ears open for the sound of armoured personnel carriers and tanks and watched for any movement from the minarets of the mosques, where the soldiers had set up posts. I was almost hyperventilating.

Eventually we made it out and back to the hotel and I had a searing hot shower, scrubbing myself clean to get rid of the smell that was in my hair and on my skin. No matter how hard I scrubbed, I could still smell it. It was still on my clothes.

I tried to sleep but was woken past midnight by a phone call from England. It was Gary, a man I'd only just begun to have a relationship with. We'd been seeing each other for the past four months and, despite the long distance and time gaps, I finally felt like I could open up my heart and trust someone again. It felt good.

He rang to tell me that his ex-girlfriend had died in a house fire. He was devastated. I listened as he told me the circumstances: she didn't have a smoke alarm in her apartment but she nearly made it to the front door before she was overcome by the smoke and died. It was horrible news and he was very upset. Even though I'd had a bad day too, I couldn't talk to him about it. The last thing he would have wanted to hear was what I'd seen that day. I listened with difficulty as he told me about this girl who I'd never known, whom he loved so much, pushing aside my own exhaustion from my overwhelming day.

The next day a smaller group of us—Rawhi, Jerome, myself and a couple other photographers—met up with Mohammed, the boy who'd helped us get into the camp the previous day, to go and see what else we could find. We were creeping along inside the camp when we heard a voice inside one of the houses. It was an old woman, calling to us from behind the screens on her windows. She was starving, she told us.

'There's no electricity, so I can't use my stove to make bread. I'm hungry, I'm hungry.' Her voice was raspy, she could barely get the words out. *Did she not even have any water?* I wondered. We only had a couple of cucumbers, which we gave to Rawhi, who was talking to her. He pushed them behind the screen for her and she snatched at them, shoving them into her mouth.

'We have to get her some food,' I said. 'We can't leave her like this.' Mohammed turned and looked at a couple of girls peering out of a window of a nearby building, giggling at the sight of the cameras.

'How can you leave an old woman to starve?' he shouted, looking up at them. 'I can give you money to get her food, why don't you just bring her a morsel, a bite, some bread, she's got nothing.' They nodded, embarrassed into silence, and said they would bring her some food. It was all so hopeless, and this was all we could do for her.

As we moved further and further inside the camp we saw more dead people. One man's body was so bloated he didn't even look human any more. He was bent over on his knees, his head touching the ground, and there were maggots crawling all over his body. We found some Red Crescent people also looking for bodies to take away. I went with one medic into a house and he counted six bodies, all men, covered with blankets. He uncovered the blankets so I could film them with the video camera I was carrying with me that day.

Some of the dead were in uniform; it looked like a dark blue colour. Worms and maggots were crawling all over them and in their scabs. And the smell. The smell made me want to vomit. I'd never inhaled anything so repugnant in my life. It's not pleasant when we leave this world, I realised. It's as ugly as we can make it.

We were turning a corner when we ran into an Israeli army ground patrol. Too late! We couldn't turn around and run away. We were busted. They asked us to show them our press cards. Mohammed, our guide, was in serious trouble. As a Palestinian who lived nearby, he wasn't a resident in the camp and the soldiers wanted to detain him. They ordered us to leave.

'We can't go and leave him,' Jerome said to the soldier. 'We've employed him. He's working for us. We'll all go, but we want him to come with us.' The soldiers had two dogs with them and a briefcase that looked like a bomb disposal kit. *They are so young*, I thought, looking at their faces. *I bet they are just as freaked out as we are*. Jenin was a tough place; thirteen soldiers had been killed in one single attack and after that they had been more on guard than before.

I didn't feel sympathy for one side or the other. I got angry at suicide bombers and the men who sent them, and I felt pity for the mothers and fathers and sisters and brothers of people who'd died on both sides of the conflict. But part of being a journalist means never taking sides. I could just as easily understand a soldier's nervousness as I could a house-bound Palestinian's despair.

'You can leave him with us. Nothing bad will happen to him,' the soldier told Jerome in perfect English.

'Do I have your word?' Jerome asked. 'We have his telephone number. We're going to call in a couple of hours to check. We'll know if something's wrong.'

'Go,' the soldier said. We left.

As we walked through someone's garden towards the edge of the camp we came across Mohammed's brother and Rawhi told him what had happened. He started crying, scared that something would happen to his brother. We didn't know what to say. When we tried Mohammed's phone later, there was no answer. We didn't see Mohammed until we returned to Jenin the next day.

We found another route in and as we began walking around we couldn't see any soldiers. *Are they cutting back on their activities now?* Mohammed said the soldiers held him for two hours and made him open house doors that were locked. If they had been booby-trapped he would have been seriously injured or killed. The Israeli army always denied doing this, but we'd heard about the practice from so many Palestinians that their denials rang hollow.

When we finally made it to the centre of the camp I realised what all the uproar was about. Before me was a bare open space, about the size of three football fields. It clearly used to be a neighbourhood but now it was just blocks of concrete, piles of cement and rubble. Who knew what was underneath it all? There were very few people moving about the area.

I walked into a building on the edge of this open space. Medics had also arrived there; they'd been told there was a body and they'd come to collect it. We climbed the stairs with them and when we got to the roof they found her in a small room there.

'Don't come in,' they said to me. 'You don't need to see.' But I could see. And worse, I could smell.

An old woman's body, which now resembled a blimp or something else equally inflated, was burnt almost beyond recognition. One of the medics was so overwhelmed by the sight he staggered out of the room for a moment to throw up.

A rocket had come through the room's window and killed her where she had stood. The medics threw a blanket over the corpse and prepared to carry her out.

I watched as they carefully carried her down the flights of stairs into the muddy slosh outside the building. There were no roads left in the middle of the camp, only mud. Then one of them yelled as he slipped and the blanket fell out of his hand and unfurled, revealing the rotting corpse to everyone who'd gathered around the pick-up truck they were using to collect the bodies. Some of the children looking on started to scream. One man vomited. As I walked away I saw the remains of something, either a human being or an animal, shredded and mixed with mud on the side of the dirt track. I felt so bad for the medics who had to approach the fly-infested corpses and haul them away.

I wasn't eating anything other than the bread and cheese Rawhi and I routinely ate every morning. Coming back to the hotel at night, I would ring Gary to see how he was coping. He would tell me how his dead ex-girlfriend had been his soul mate, the love of his life, and how they had belonged together. It hurt me to hear this, but I tried not to let him know that. There was so much I couldn't tell Gary.

I couldn't tell him that that very morning, as we parked the hard car and I climbed out, a bullet whizzed past my head, sweeping so close over my hair that I felt it. I couldn't tell him that I wasn't eating because I was waking every morning at dawn, driving for hours to find a way into a camp where I would spend the next few hours counting the mangled and rotting remains of what were once people. I couldn't tell him that I awoke at three in the morning still smelling the rot of dead people on my skin and in my hair, even after taking scalding hot showers. I couldn't tell him that I needed to lean on him, that I was having trouble dealing with what I was seeing. That I needed to know there was more to life than this senseless waste of humanity. It was too much.

Everything began to take a toll on me. I would sit silently in the hard car as we rambled over rocky paths and through fields, trying the same routes that had got us in over the past few days only to find them blocked, then trying a different path. Our little band of journalists drove through a national forest and found contractors working on a road, guarded by Israeli border police. We climbed out to take a break. Jerome took some pictures of the men working and I started talking to the man supervising the contractors. He had a handgun tucked into the back of his trousers.

'What's all this?' I asked him.

'It's the new fence,' he said. I'd heard about the separation barrier, but it seemed to be just talk. Sharon was discussing building a fence to separate the West Bank from Israel, to stop suicide bombers from coming in and blowing themselves up along with Israeli civilians. So far, that's all it was—talk.

'How long you been working on this?' I asked the man.

'Since January.'

'You're kidding.' I looked around. 'Where's the Green Line?' I asked. He pointed to a field about a hundred metres away. They'd taken an extra hundred metres of Palestinian land to build the fence.

While I was in Jenin, Ramallah was still being hit hard. Marwan Barghouti was arrested and taken away. *They actually took him*, I thought. I was surprised. Shimon Peres said he would be tried in an open court; Israel was accusing him of orchestrating shooting attacks that killed many

Israelis as well as a Greek Orthodox monk. Meanwhile, I was looking for bodies of Palestinians during the day and breaking up with Gary at night. Everything was a mess. I was a mess.

Elizabeth had arrived to take over photography duties from Jerome and she sat in sympathetic silence as I cried during our drives into the camp. The military was scaling back its presence and becoming more permissive with the press. We still had to sneak in to the camp on foot, parking the car nearby, but we could leave Jenin in our cars through the proper exits. It never made sense, but none of this did.

One evening, as Elizabeth and I drove out of Jenin's main entrance we were stopped at an Israeli checkpoint and the soldiers wanted to check our press cards. I was permanently tense, so the slightest thing would set me off. This was an unnecessary delay. I yelled at the soldier, showed him my press card and told Elizabeth to keep driving, muttering something about men and what a pain in the backside they were. Elizabeth turned to the soldier and said to him, 'She's breaking up with her boyfriend, and you're a guy. She doesn't much like guys right now.' He let us pass.

The next day when we left the camp through the same checkpoint the same soldier was manning the post. After checking our press cards he looked at me and asked, 'So, you still hate men today?'

'Yes!' I snapped back, smothering a small smile.

After days of diplomatic toing and froing, the military closures in most of the Palestinian towns were eased. The tanks pulled out of the centre of Jenin to the outskirts. More press came in and were able to move around with some ease. I ventured to the hospital to finally try and get some idea of how many people had died and I spoke with Mahmoud Abu Ghali, the director of the hospital in Jenin refugee camp. I sat in his office and listened as he described the Palestinians being massacred by the Israelis.

'You didn't see the refrigerators?' he asked me.

'What refrigerators?' I replied.

'The refrigerators that they put all the corpses in. Trucks with fridges inside to keep the bodies cool.' There was no way I could now verify what he was saying. The Israelis absolutely denied reports of these types of accusations.

'Do you mind if I check with your registration office downstairs for the numbers?' I asked him.

'Of course, go ahead.' I went downstairs to the registration office and poked my head in the door.

'Do you mind if I ask you some questions?' I asked the men inside.

'Welcome, welcome,' they said, holding the door open and asking me to sit down. We drew up a list of everyone who'd died before the Israelis moved in and of those who had died afterwards. How many bodies came in, who they were, and when they had arrived. There had been about an eight-day period when the hospital was unable to send staff out to collect bodies because Israeli forces had surrounded the hospital. This I knew because we saw the tanks and Armoured Personnel Carriers (APCs) outside the hospital's walls, preventing anyone from entering or even going near. After we counted every body bag and every bag of body bits we reached a total that was way below what everyone was saying—about 50 in the end. Less than the toll in Nablus, which was about 80.

After all that rhetoric, all that anger, all those rumours,

these 50 dead would now seem unimportant to the rest of the world because they were much fewer than the 500 dead everyone had been talking about. After all our fervour to cover the story it now appeared there were no piles of hundreds of bodies. We'd been misled.

I was ready to leave by then. I'd been covering Jenin's dead for nigh on two weeks and I was exhausted. I was tired of the Palestinians and the Israelis and their conflicting versions of events. Tired of stiffening at the sight of a soldier with a gun. Tired of losing my temper at Palestinian doctors and Israeli border police. Damaged at heart over the death of a woman I never knew and her effect on the man I was falling in love with. I was struggling to maintain energy and interest in a story that was consuming me, taking away my appetite and keeping me up at night with memories and smells of rotting flesh. I was beginning to forget what the rest of the world felt like. Beginning to forget that humanity, so palpably missing here, still existed in the world and that I shouldn't lose heart.

CHAPTER SIXTEEN

Ramallah
14 November 2004

the crowds started whistling, the high-pitched sound grew stronger and stronger.

'What are they whistling at?' I asked my colleagues, watching from our rooftop position.

'The helicopters are coming,' one friend said.

I squinted into the bright blue skyline and tried to see something, anything, but I couldn't. I smiled. Trust Palestinians to be able to spot helicopters before everyone else. They were so used to the Israeli airborne rocket attacks . . . of course they'd know. I still couldn't see them, but the whirr of the rotor blades grew louder and louder.

'They're behind the buildings now,' my colleague pointed over my shoulder.

I tried to focus until they finally came into view. There were four of them: two enormous Egyptian helicopters and two Israeli Apaches. The Apaches hovered as the Egyptian choppers descended in a swirl of dust and debris, garbage flying in the air that had turned orange from the dust. I wondered how the Israelis felt about having the Egyptians intrude so far inside their airspace—normally a gross violation of their security.

Palestinian police fired round after round in the air, uselessly trying to keep the people away from the choppers. The crowds continued to surge towards them. It was chaos: the yelling, the whistling, the roar of the choppers, the dust filling my nostrils and getting in my eyes. The gunfire was relentless. My eardrums started to throb. We ducked behind speakers and cameras as bullets fired into the compound snapped near us, some 50 metres away.

I thought the helicopters would take off and leave. I thought the Palestinians now in charge—Mahmoud Abbas, Ahmed Qurei—would postpone the funeral until the next day, after the crowd had left. I thought someone might try to get the masses to pray. A hundred thousand Palestinian men on their knees in silence was the best way I could think of to quickly and peacefully sedate everyone. I didn't think they would go ahead with the funeral right then and there.

Men were crammed up against the doors of the choppers. *How on earth are they going to open the doors against that pressure?* I wondered. I could see some of those inside furiously waving the men away. Mere moments felt like an intractable forever. *This isn't going anywhere.* Then, incredibly, a pick-up truck swept through the crowd, which parted before it like the Red Sea for Moses. When it reached one of the helicopters, the doors opened and the policemen on the tray of the truck jumped off and collected the coffin from the helicopter. Draped in a Palestinian flag, it was lowered onto the back of the truck, which took off through the throng.

Is this it? Would this be the mad dash to Jerusalem? Throughout the night before, Palestinians swore they would take Arafat and bury him in Jerusalem, where he always said he wanted to be laid to rest.

'Let them shoot at us, thousands of us, coming towards the checkpoint, they'll have a massacre on their hands,' the young men cried to me as we stood outside the compound walls on the eve of the funeral. Posters of Arafat were pasted on the walls, and the candles set up outside the gate gave his mottled face a yellow glow. There was no anger that night, only grief. But the headlong rush to Jerusalem wasn't going to happen. Israel would never agree, however adamant the men were. I watched to see whether the pick-up truck would careen out of the compound, but it remained hemmed in by the crowd.

There was no formality to this funeral. Maybe it started with the whirr of the choppers, maybe it started with the pick-up truck's ramshackle drive over the red carpet laid out in the morning for a proper reception. The Palestinians grieved the only way they knew how after all these years — with chants, shouts, fingers thrusting in the air, people stomping over each other in a frenzy to reach the coffin and touch Arafat one last time.

We watched as Palestinian policemen fired shots in the air, shouting, willing the crowds to take up their cry: 'With our souls, our blood, we'll redeem you, Abu Ammar.' The people called on their fallen leader. They cried. They fired in the air. Their faces were red from crying and red from pushing and shoving each other in the massive crowd.

The truck carrying the coffin went around and around the compound before stopping at one side, near the burial site underneath some tall trees.

'That's it,' one of the cameramen on the roof with me murmured. 'He's in the ground.'

As I watched the feverish swirl of men and dust I wondered how Arafat would have felt, whether he could have ever predicted that it would end for him like this. For so long he'd danced with the devil, pushing both his people and those of Israel to the limit, but for what gain? His people were still as isolated as he had been, trapped in the confines of the West Bank.

By most accounts, he hadn't even slept in his room, which had been hit by Israeli gunfire during the siege of September 2002. His most loyal followers slept in the building with him. Palestinian police bunked on the ground floor in small rooms darkened by the sandbags stashed against the windows and with their laundry hanging from lines inside their makeshift dorms. Whoever had wanted to see Arafat had had to traipse through the checkpoints, swerve past the barrels filled with cement posted in the middle of the helipad in the compound to prevent any Israeli helicopters from landing there, duck behind the sandbagged entrance and climb to the third floor past his aide, Nabil Abu Rdeneh's, cramped office. Everyone from Colin Powell to foreign activists made that trek.

I remembered the first time I met Arafat. I was in Gaza, it was May 2001, and I was with a group of Palestinian journalists outside his seaside compound. We were waiting for him to return from a trip to Egypt. I was introduced to Mohammed Eddayeh, his moustachioed bodyguard, who'd become famous simply because there was rarely a photograph taken of Arafat then that didn't have him in it. There was a joke doing the rounds that Eddayeh would pull up photographers and ask them why they always included 'that man in the keffiyeh' whenever they took pictures of him. He had inherited his job from his father, who was killed in Tunis in 1985 when the Israelis bombed the PLO headquarters there. Arafat, who'd had a lucky escape, took Eddayeh in, practically adopting him. Eddayeh had worked for him ever since.

As we sat there waiting in the compound, I had noticed all the shiny Chevrolet Jeeps and Mercedes in the car park and wondered who they belonged to and who had paid for them.

'There's a story in that,' a colleague said, after noticing my focus. 'All the money Arafat gets, where does it go? Who sees it? What does it pay for?' All along Arafat was accused of corruption, of pocketing millions in aid and assistance meant for the Palestinians, for their infrastructure, their schools and hospitals. Gaza was still mostly sandy roads; there was no proper sewage system, especially in the refugee camps, and people still received water from tankers that drove slowly through the streets playing music like ice cream vans. So where had all the money gone?

I was snapped out of my thoughts by the sound of screaming tyres: Arafat had arrived. The policemen jumped out of the cars of the motorcade before the vehicles had stopped, in what I thought was a completely unnecessary show of manliness. Eddayeh went around to the passenger door of the first car and leant inside, taking Arafat's gun from him—Arafat used to say that he carried the gun because he didn't feel safe when he passed the Israeli settlements and checkpoints on the way to Gaza City. Arafat walked slowly past the honour guard that only moments before had been nonchalantly lounging in the shade and scamming cigarettes off journalists. As Arafat wandered over to the journalists, they scrambled to position themselves around him. Many knelt at his feet with microphones and tape recorders in their hands.

I stood back with Adel Hana, an AP photographer in Gaza, and Ahmed Jadallah, his Reuters counterpart, and watched the spectacle. Arafat made a couple of statements— he'd often employ the same slogans as a comment in reaction to an Israeli manoeuvre or statement, some of them so predictable we would recite them ourselves: 'Whoever doesn't like it can go and drink from the Dead Sea,' or, 'Oh mountain, don't let the wind shake you.' Then he looked up, noticing me. Adel and Ahmed jostled behind me, placing a camera lens on each of my shoulders to get a direct shot.

'Jamie, he likes you. He's looking at you. It means he wants you to ask him a question,' Adel said into my ear. I chuckled and continued to watch. I had nothing to ask of Arafat.

From my point of view Arafat seemed fixated only on his own survival. I was convinced he didn't want to lose his status as an international representative for the Palestinians. He didn't want to lose his privileges. He didn't want to give up the image of being a revolutionary freedom fighter for that of leader of a tiny bit of land. He'd let thousands die; I didn't believe he really cared. Whether he had any more cards left to play or not didn't matter. He took his uncompromising stand with him to his grave.

I thought that Sharon, too, was more interested in his place in the history books than in the daily dangers his people confronted. I believed that in his mind his legacy was more important—that it didn't matter if a few thousand Jews died to achieve his ultimate goal of Greater Israel. History would judge those deaths as a necessary and important sacrifice for the survival of the Jewish people. I could have been wrong, but that was my feeling then.

Indeed, even when Arafat was confined to Ramallah, he refused to pass over control to others who had a better chance of improving the Palestinians' lot. He continually sabotaged Mahmoud Abbas' attempts to implement changes, restricted his powers, prevented access to financial statements, insisted he still be involved in negotiations and that no one, but no one, was the leader of the Palestinians except him. He would not accept any kind of symbolic position; he would never be an honorary president. He was in charge and he would remain so until he died, no matter what happened to the Palestinians.

And so it came to pass. Even when he was whisked away to France for medical treatment, frail and sickly, Arafat refused to appoint a successor. When he died, speculation mounted over who would replace him. Would it be Abbas, the man in the background who never sought publicity, or would it be Marwan Barghouti, now in jail and serving five life sentences? The concept that Barghouti would ever be freed to take part in Palestinian elections prompted furious denials from the Israeli government. Although in my mind, it was a possibility.

Barghouti didn't allow anyone to defend him in court; he decried the court's legitimacy and said it had no jurisdiction over him, a member of the Palestinian parliament. He claimed a publicised letter from Israel's attorney-general, calling him a 'first-rate architect of terrorism', tainted the fairness of his trial before it even got underway. It wasn't completely unlikely that, if he were to challenge the court's verdict, he might have a chance at having the entire process declared a mistrial and then be freed. Barghouti was always a moderate who believed in a two-state solution, someone who wanted a peaceful solution to the conflict, despite his militant connections. I would never rule out Israel releasing him from prison to allow him to take part in future elections, since his popularity would only increase the longer he remained behind bars.

❧

But in the end, what had Arafat achieved for the Palestinians? They were locked into their towns when he died and their economy was in ruins. When I saw my old Palestinian friends again I couldn't ask them how 'the situation' was because it was obvious the situation was bad. Nothing had improved since I left nearly two years before.

Ultimately Abbas won the election held on 9 January 2005 — my 30th birthday. *What kind of mandate will he have? What sort of respect will he be able to command among militant groups?*

Unlike Arafat in his combat fatigues, Abbas always wears a suit. He looks like a dry accountant, not a charismatic prime minister. He exudes an almost tangible disdain for the media and always appears uncomfortable when confronted with the glare of television lights and camera flashes. But he has been able to do what Arafat had not: meet with Sharon and declare an end to violence.

Sharon, to his credit, would not budge from his determination to withdraw Israelis from the Gaza Strip despite the opposition from within the ranks of his right-wing Likud Party. He spoke of the 'painful concessions' Israel was making by returning control of Jericho to the Palestinians. It made me laugh in a way, since Jericho and much of the West Bank was under Palestinian control when I first arrived there in September 2000. A painful concession to Sharon was agreeing to go back to the original guidelines the peace proposals were based on. But it was progress. *Progress!* There's that word again.

Former Israeli Prime Minister Ehud Barak said in January 2001, when the talks collapsed and his leadership was finished, 'In a few years, we will bury our hundreds of dead, and they will bury their thousands of dead, and we will go back to the negotiating table, and we will face the same issues.'

He was right.

Palestine Hotel, Baghdad, Iraq
14 February 2005

I t was damn cold in the AP office. Even with the heater on full blast next to my chair and wearing a scarf and two sweaters, I was still freezing. This was not good. I couldn't concentrate on the computer screen in front of me and the tome I was trying to punch out. Iraqi politicians were wheeling and dealing for positions in the new government with all the panache and savvy of Western diplomats. After reporting endless bombings and kidnappings and killings, the story was finally beginning to interest me again.

It was almost surreal that I was back here again, in the Middle East. I'd just relocated to Cairo—my next posting with the AP—and only two days after signing the lease on my new apartment I flew to Amman to get an Iraqi visa. Less than two weeks in the region and I was already back in Baghdad. This war zone thing was really beginning to be a pattern in my life.

We were in virtual lockdown in the Palestine Hotel; the security situation was so bad we couldn't go out except for interviews and media briefings. Kidnappings, beheadings, random bombings, danger all around and still I could not stay away. This really was it, wasn't it? My life as a war correspondent was on a one-way track and I couldn't get off.

As I tapped away at my keyboard Al-Arabiya television flashed that there'd been an explosion in Beirut. A big one. *It's not the first time*, I thought, dismissing it. It was probably some Hezbollah guy killed in a car bomb. But this one is really big, one of my colleagues told me. The news report was of nine dead.

I looked up at the TV screen to see cars on fire—a man, his clothes aflame, was stuck in the passenger door of a burning car, trying to get out. Another man was on his knees, his head nearly touching the ground in front of him as a man stood over him trying to put out the flames on his back and shoulders. I winced as I watched the scenes. One of the translators came in and said that Rafik Hariri, the former prime minister, had been killed in the blast. Then the memories came flooding back.

I was in Lebanon when President Rene Mouawad was killed in November 1989. By that time we'd been stuck in the little village of Atchany for eight months. No school, no travel. Mouawad, like Hariri, was in a car and the bomb had detonated as he passed. There was another bomb waiting just around the corner in case the first one didn't work. Mouawad, his driver and bodyguards were all killed.

I remembered the Lebanese blamed Syria then, as they did now. I remembered how that was only one moment of terror in a slate of many. I remembered how my father didn't like to line up at bakeries to buy bread because they were targeted with car bombs. I remembered the rocket fired at my grandparents' building that obliterated one of the floors.

The street scene I now watched on the TV reminded me of downtown east Beirut, where my mother used to take us shopping, passing men with stalls of bread rolls filled with zaatar. The smell of the zaatar, the kanafe, the food I loved and missed, came back to me. I remembered the colours of the city and the Lebanese accents that spoke to me on a level that an Iraqi, Palestinian or Egyptian voice never could. It reminded me of my aunts smothering my face in their enormous cleavages as they hugged me hello. It was always so hard to breathe in there.

The well-dressed Lebanese men crying on television reminded me of the boys who used to greet us as we walked by on summer nights along with everyone else in the mountain towns.

'Bonsoir, mademoiselle,' they used to say and try to offer us flowers. We'd always giggle our refusals and walk on, looking for ice cream.

Suddenly I was fourteen again and all that bewilderment, all that fear, washed over me. I felt my stomach turn. But this time I knew more, I knew better. I was stronger now. I rang Sydney to speak to my parents in case they were watching the news. They weren't. Some sitcom was on and they were having a quiet evening. I didn't tell them about it. I knew they'd hear all about it the next day. Let at least this evening pass untroubled for them.

I still felt like a fourteen-year-old in one respect though: I hadn't told them I was in Baghdad. I was hoping the ten remaining days I would be here would pass quietly and they would never have to know. Otherwise they'd worry. An Italian journalist had been kidnapped and she was filmed begging for her life. My parents didn't need the extra worry. We endured our time in Lebanon together so long ago, and here I was again placing myself in danger. I couldn't bear to tell them and that made me feel like a naughty little girl again, afraid of their disapproval.

Lebanon was my first experience of war, of blood and death and bombs. Of hatred and division and power struggles at the expense of destiny and life. Then there was Jerusalem and its intractable hold on two diametrically opposed brethren. And now Iraq, a new war, a new reality in this post-September 11 world. *Who knows what will happen in Lebanon now. Would the Syrians actually finally leave? And me, would I want to be there to watch it happen?* I was already feeling that journalistic tug to be there, in the thick of it.

The US recalled its ambassador from Syria and the world condemned the attack. *But is any of this really new? In reality it is only history repeating itself.*

Nothing had changed, except me.